THE witch's
Wheel
OF THE
Year

Publisher
Balthazar Pagani

Graphic design, layout, and editing
Bebung

Vivida

Vivida® is a registered trademark property of White Star s.r.l.

Piazzale Luigi Cadorna, 6
20123 Milano, Italia
www.whitestar.it

Translation: Contextus S.r.l., Pavia (Christine Guthry)
Editing: Phillip Gaskill

ISBN 978-88-544-2151-6
1 2 3 4 5 6   29 28 27 26 25

Printed in China

Federica Vanini

The Witch's Wheel of the Year

CELEBRATING THE SEASONS
THROUGH NATURE, MAGIC,
AND FOLKLORE

ILLUSTRATIONS BY
Erica Brucoli

Vivida

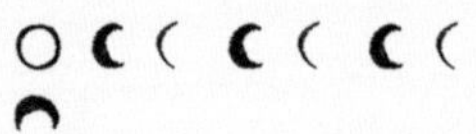

Contents

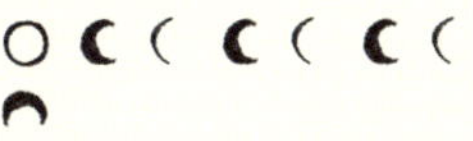

Imbolc: to be reborn, I let go

✦ 51 ✦

FOCUS
Sacrifice and purification

ENERGIES PRESENT
Independent thinking

SELF-EVALUATION
The connection of the spirit

MAGIC AND SPELLS
The magic of transformation

RITES OF PASSAGE
The path from Imbolc to Ostara

Ostara: the rebirth of the 'true self'

✦ 69 ✦

FOCUS
With strong roots it is time to bloom

ENERGIES PRESENT
Balance and introspection

SELF-EVALUATION
I am the seed, what will help me blossom?

MAGIC AND SPELLS
I allow energy to bloom

RITES OF PASSAGE
The path from Ostara to Beltane

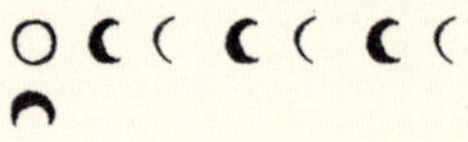

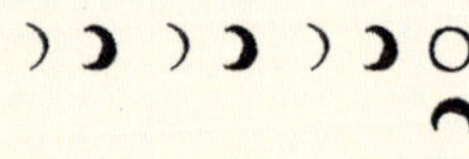

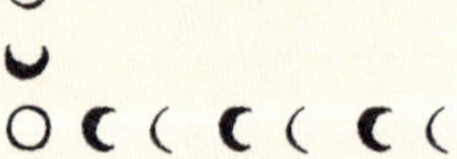

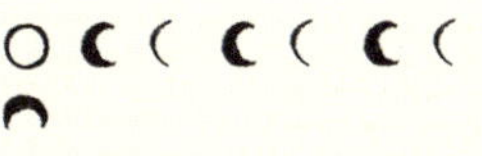  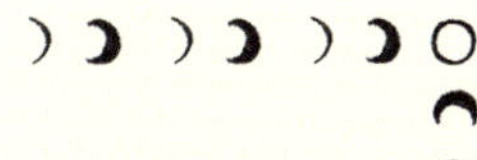

Introduction

Around us, time seems to flow inexorably. How often have we felt disconnected?

Our frenetic lifestyle, with its demands on productivity and efficiency, has led us to accumulate things and money, but to lack a sense of fulfilment so that, when we finally stop this feverish pace to notice what is around us, we feel lost and empty.

Increasingly more people are realizing that, over time, we have lost touch with Mother Nature. Inside our castles of concrete and asphalt, we remain deaf to her calling and blind to her unspoiled beauty.

So, how can we bridge this gap?

That is what I asked myself many years ago, when I began my spiritual journey. Through time, I learned a secret that totally changed my life: the natural realm is not as far out of reach as we think, provided we are ready to acknowledge its significance and sacredness.

YULE
Winter Solstice
IMBOLC
Candlemas
OSTARA
Spring equinox
BELTANE
May Day
LITHA
Summer solstice
LAMMAS
Lunasa
MABON
Fall equinox
SAMHAIN
Halloween
WINTER
SPRING
SUMMER
FALL

Everything in nature is perfect and has its own rhythm, evolution, purpose, and end. This awareness allows every living being to exist in connection with everything that surrounds it and, even if we have forgotten it, this includes us.

In centuries past, before the onset of modern society, humans were an integral part of this interconnectedness.

Prehistoric peoples lived in a symbiotic relationship with nature and totally depended on it.

This central role gave rise to a magical and religious vision of the powers of nature and the idea that, to live peacefully, actively participating in the transformative process of things was key.

Despite time appearing to flow linearly into the future, nature teaches us that existence evolves in a cyclical fashion. The passing seasons gift us with the experience of life, of transformations and endings.

Everything around us changes and this influences our body, our mood, and our personal energy.

The knowledge of this cycle is contained within the Wheel of the Year, a modern interpretation of the ancient traditions linked to agrarian rituals and celebrations of solar events.

Initially introduced by the scholar Jacob Grimm and later defined by the neopagan movement of the 20th century, the Wheel of the Year is an opportunity to reconnect with nature, rediscover the value of seasonal cycles, and connect with the cosmos.

The solar year consists of eight stages known as sabbats: Samhain, Imbolc, Beltane, and Lammas are the major sabbats, which represent the key times of transformation in the natural realm; while the minor sabbats Yule, Ostara, Litha, and Mabon represent the solar events of solstices and equinoxes.

Each festival is rich in symbolisms, traditions, and teachings. Knowing and celebrating them gives us the opportunity to relive ancient traditions by embarking on a path of personal and spiritual growth.

Following this path has changed my life profoundly, giving me the strength to rise above an existence I felt I had outgrown.

The Wheel of the Year is not an exclusive path for a select few: it is an enchanted world in which the passing of time is an opportunity to understand ourselves and our surroundings at a deeper level.

This book outlines a path that will take you on an extraordinary exploration, in which you will learn about the history, the traditions, and the vibrations that resonate with your soul.

Along this journey, you will not only be a reader, but an active protagonist who will have the chance to practice spells, experiencing firsthand the magic of the year.

Are you ready to cross the threshold?

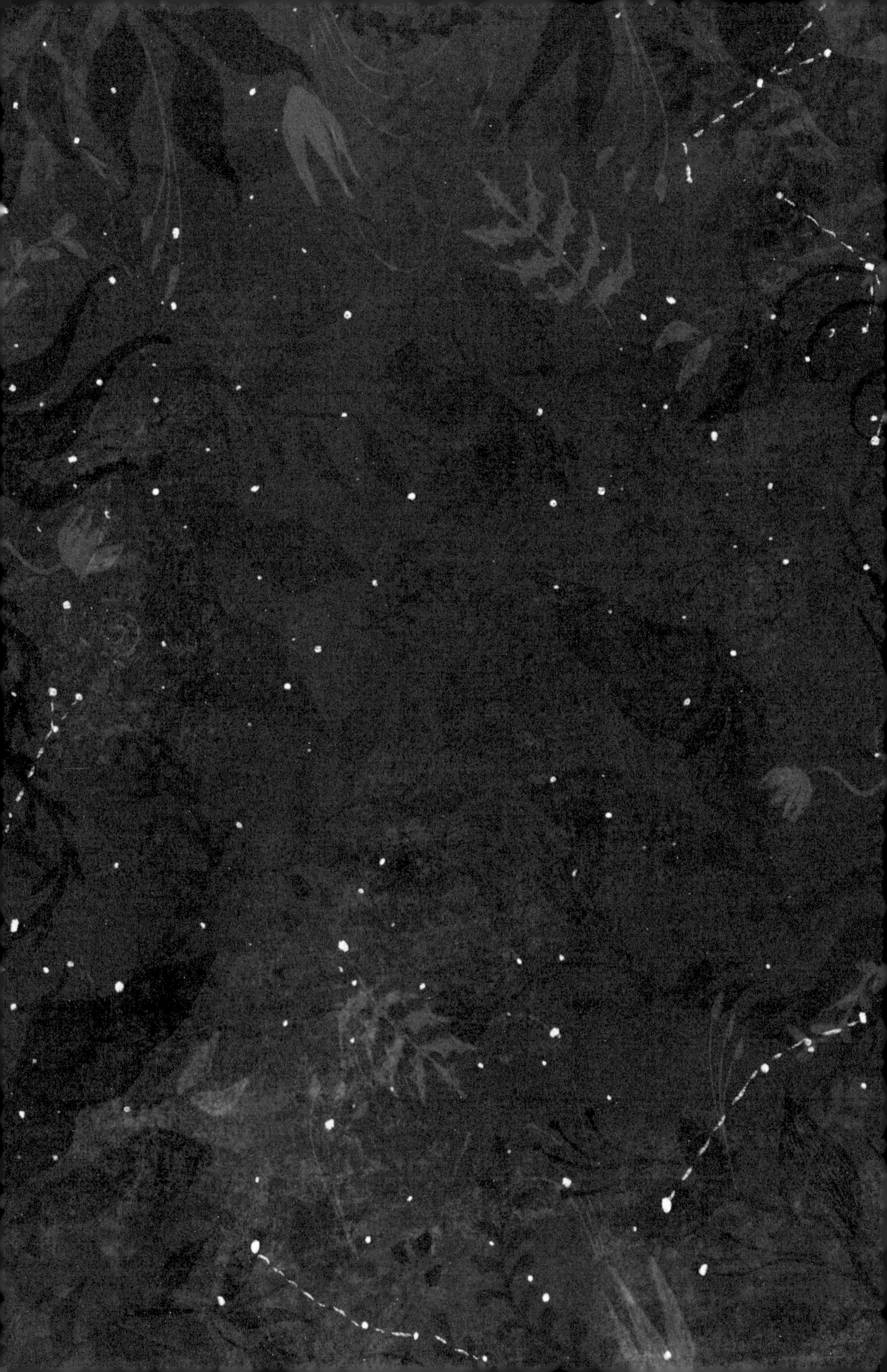

Samhain

✦ ✦ ✦

Halloween

OCTOBER 31—NOVEMBER 1–2

My soul and my roots

✦ ✦ ✦

THE LAST HARVEST FESTIVAL is named Samhain, from the Gaelic *samhuinn*, which means *summer's end*, which for the Celtic peoples coincided with the New Year.

Besides being at the center of today's Halloween holiday, Samhain bears a fascinating connection to various traditions around the world, in which the themes of commemorating the dead, and the merging of this world and the afterlife, are a common thread.

The veil separating the underworld from that of the living dissolves, allowing the spirits to get in touch with the human dimension.

This magical event has a double meaning: on one hand, there's the joy of celebrating one's ancestors; on the other, the fear that malevolent spirits could harm people or crops.

Although rooted in pre-Christian traditions originating from different European cultures, the Day of the Dead celebration has fascinating links with Samhain, such as celebrating the ancestors. The most common ritual consists of preparing a feast to honor the dead.

Families gather to cook their loved ones' favorite meals, reserving a symbolic place at the table for incorporeal guests. Next to the table, a small altar is set up to commemorate those who are no longer with us. On it are displayed photos, flowers, and other significant objects to remember them.

Through these simple actions, Samhain reveals its secrets to us: we are the result of our ancestors' choices and behaviors and we will be forever tethered to them by a thread that traverses cultures and ages. This connection nourishes our soul with a sense of stability and belonging.

The absence of light

✦ ✦ ✦

Born in the bronze shades of twilight at a time when the Wheel of the Year celebrates life's cyclical nature: the inevitable decline of summer days and the coming winter cold.

Samhain's magic leads us into the depths of an underground cave where we shall face our innermost darkness.

The setting of the Sun on October 31 marks the beginning of a profound transformative cycle that will affect us physically and spiritually.

The absence of light and the colder, damper temperatures provide the ideal conditions for roots to take hold and, similarly, the human soul is called upon to ground its spirit and become wiser.

The Wheel of the Year teaches us that the word 'end' is only part of a larger picture. The fruit that falls from the tree and rots doesn't cease to exist: rather, it nourishes a new, vital cycle. Likewise, we too are part of such universal powers.

This view of continuity allows us to understand and accept that even this phase of darkness is necessary for our evolution.

In the same way that we embrace the Sun's radiating energy at its peak, we need the courage to delve into the deepest waters of our soul, into the place where we hide our wounds, our pain, and the cuts we have slowly mended with great effort. It is precisely by nurturing this aspect of our soul that we can truly be reborn at the end of each cycle: such is the profound lesson that the water sign Scorpio teaches us as the guardian of this time of year.

Awareness is the key for authentic renewal, enabling us to dig deep within ourselves, not limiting ourselves to superficial analysis.

Fear of change

✦ ✦ ✦

THE MONTH'S ENERGY

November teaches us that negatively perceiving some energies and situations, often labeled as "heavy," stems from our fears. We fear the unknown, the subconscious, death, and endings, and we project such fears onto that which surrounds us. However, a spiritual view of this phase of the year acknowledges the cyclical nature of all energy, guiding us toward a deeper awakening through the awareness that nothing vanishes, but everything changes, integrating into a different stage of existence, then returning to the endless cycle, all of which includes our actions.

FULL MOON

This month's full Moon bears a particularly complicated energy and puts us to the test. Its milky light can lighten our path, allowing us to recuperate.

During this phase, we seek the Moon's help to restore our strength.

We connect to its power and let it awaken our spirit. This is why, during a full Moon, you should place a silver pendant outside to charge it with its energy throughout the night. Feel the Moon's power flow through you as you wear this charm.

NEW MOON

The month of Samhain, in association with the new Moon, gives us the chance to deeply cleanse our energy field by ridding it of the negativity accrued thus far.

During this phase, you may perform some cleansing rituals.

For this purpose, we'll use a Selenite crystal, the energy of which is considered to be calming and cleansing. It is believed to help dispel negative energy and assist in meditation.

During the night, place it outside, then cleanse yourself by moving the crystal counter-clockwise all over your body in circular motions.

I slowly take my steps

✦ ✦ ✦

Samhain symbolizes the Celtic New Year; this phase of new beginnings, which is charged with energy, can be confusing. That is why, to be able to face our journey in complete consciousness, we need to understand the direction we are taking.

Concentrate and answer the questions that most resonate with your soul.

✦ ***To cleanse your body of negative energy, you take a bath with essential oils and dried flowers. What ingredients do you choose?***

A. Almond milk, vanilla essence, and rose petals.
B. Eucalyptus essential oil, orange blossoms, and dried sage.

✦ ***Imagine possessing a magic power. What gift would you choose to transform your life and the world around you?***

A. Clairvoyance, to be able to make decisions wisely.
B. Telekinesis, to be able to move objects as I please.

✦ ***Universal wisdom is revealed to us through phrases that we read or hear by chance. Of the following, which one resonates the most with your inner self?***

A. The biggest gift is appreciating life and the magic around you.
B. We define our own destiny: every action and thought changes reality.

✦ ***Do you usually prefer to make your spells:***

A. At night when it's quiet, so you can concentrate on every action and every whisper.
B. During a sunny day, to practice outside and let yourself be guided by the power of nature.

✦ ***Imagine an ancient chest with mother-of-pearl inlays, shrouded in an aura of mystery. Carefully stored within are the objects you will use in your magic practice. What do you find?***

A. Your magic herbs with their intoxicating essences, books, and colored candles.
B. The magic cauldron in which your spells come to life, your crystals, and fragrant incense.

YOU ANSWERED MOSTLY "A":
SLOW AND DELIBERATE STEPS

True strength resides in calm, thoughtfulness, and balance

✦ ✦ ✦

The spirit animal that could be your guide is the turtle.

Turtle is frequently associated with wisdom, due to its longevity and ability to observe the world calmly and with detachment. Its shell represents inner wisdom, which allows us to face life's challenges in a calm and balanced way. Like the turtle retreating into its shell to think and protect itself, you too ought to find time for meditation and introspection, because true strength lies not in speed, but rather in patience, perseverance, and balance.

Learning to tap into your wisdom in your daily choices is the key to success.

Advised practice: the key to my soul.

YOU ANSWERED MOSTLY "B":

YOU ALLOW YOURSELF TO BE GUIDED BY YOUR ENTHUSIASM

Life is an exciting journey full of opportunities to be seized

✦ ✦ ✦

The spirit animal that could be your guide is the energetic hare.

The hare is famous for its speed and its ability to escape predators. This characteristic makes it a symbol of alertness, quick reflexes, and the ability to seize opportunities on the fly. Like the hare that springs at the first sign of danger, we too should be ready to adapt to changing situations and react just as swiftly to life's challenges. We must learn to decipher the signals that the universe is sending us, and to follow our intuition to make the best decisions. Apply your skills and power to both your life and your magic practice and allow yourself to be guided by your feelings, because your limitless personal power can help you achieve all your goals.

Advised practice: pushing back on evil.

Beyond the threshold of the invisible

✦ ✦ ✦

Because of its connection with the darkest energies of the year, nowadays Samhain is still regarded with fear—although the rituals, for the most part, are steeped in ancient folk practices for warding off negativity and celebrating change.

CONNECTION: THE SHRINE OF THE ANCESTORS

Celebrating one's ancestors plays a central role in the daily rituals and magic practices of different cultures around the world. Some of these ancestral customs have been abandoned, leading to a great loss. This bond allows us to connect with our roots.

SUPPLIES: A lantern with a candle, symbols of our ancestors (e.g., photos, mementos, or a sheet of paper with their names), a glass of wine or liqueur, incense.

METHOD: When using photos, it is vital to ascertain that they do not depict anyone alive, or they will need to be cut out or discarded.

Choose a spot in your home to devote to your ancestors. Carefully position all the objects by placing photos or symbolic objects at the center.

Light the incense and diffuse the smoke, then light the candle inside the lantern.

Now it is time to establish your links. Therefore, you should recite the following spell:

Your blood flows within me,
from you to me time travels,
ancestors listen to my call,
I, (say your name), your guidance and support seek.

You can perform this ritual as often as you like. It will help you establish an ever-deeper bond with your ancestors.

INTROSPECTION: THE KEY TO MY SOUL

The key is often used in magic as an object to "open" or "close" specific energies. By blessing this pendant, you can use it to more easily access the energies in your magic practice, and for your spiritual awakening.

SUPPLIES: A pendant in the shape of a key, a bowl of water, lavender flowers, white chalk, a black cloth.

METHOD: After sunset, spread the black cloth before you and use the chalk to draw a pentacle, a symbol of strength and protection. At the center, place the bowl filled with crystal-clear water, in which you will dip your pendant and the lavender flowers.

Close your eyes and breathe deeply. Visualize a bright, warm, and radiant light like the Sun's emanating from your chest. Imagine this light flowing through your arms and hands and reaching the pendant immersed in the water. Feel the energy connecting with the pendant, creating an invisible, yet powerful, bond.

Now slowly recite your spell:

Key to the worlds,
provide access to my magic.
With you today, I call upon my soul.
Guide my awakening.

Allow the pendant to lie in the water for 24 hours to fully absorb the magic energy you summoned. After this time, take it out and dry it thoroughly. Now it's ready to be worn to amplify your magic power.

PROTECTION: PUSHING BACK ON EVIL

The mirror is an everyday object, yet it can be used effectively in protection spells by taking advantage of its reflective surface.

SUPPLIES: A mirror, a sheet of paper, a pencil, a black candle, incense.

METHOD: After carefully washing and purifying the surface of the mirror under running water, and spreading incense smoke along its entire surface, write a sentence expressing the protection you seek on the sheet of paper. The words must be specific, stating who or what you want to keep out of your life.

Fold the paper in four and place it on the back of the mirror (on the non-reflective side).

Light the candle and, being very careful, begin to slowly let the wax drip on the paper. Cover the entire paper in wax so that it is tightly sealed onto the back of the mirror. Be careful not to burn yourself; to be safer, use a toothpick in order to not touch the wax.

As you go, mentally recite your protection spell:

Protective mirror, reflect evil,
be impassable, and back it will have to go.
Be like a shield, strong and secure,
against every threat, an impenetrable wall.

After completing the ritual, your mirror is ready to be hung in your home with the reflective surface facing outward toward a window or door, at your own discretion.

The path from Samhain to Yule

✦ ✦ ✦

THE TRANSITION FROM ONE FESTIVAL TO ANOTHER begins during the month of November, when we find ourselves before a path distinguished above all by the energy of Scorpio, which is ruled by Pluto, god of the underworld and transformation. This phase symbolizes our descent into the depths of the subconscious and the subsequent ascent to a higher consciousness.

***By nurturing this part of our soul,
we can truly love ourselves and evolve.***

Scorpio is the sign of a dual nature: on the one hand, it symbolizes passion and the ability to face challenges; on the other, its ability to regenerate itself signifies transformation.

We are at the mercy of an eternal waltz, and every day we learn new steps. With every cycle we rise from our ashes like the phoenix, which is the deep lesson we are being taught; and with this wisdom, we move forward.

***The main theme of this phase is:
We cannot complain about the world's problems
if we are a cog in that undoing.***

Here's what you can do to live correctly and learn how to control this power:

- ✦ Meditate while looking at the flame of a candle.
- ✦ Place four bags of salt around your bed for protection.
- ✦ Before bed, sip a relaxing herbal tea with chamomile, lemon balm, and lavender.
- ✦ Plan your day and celebrate your wins.
- ✦ Carry cloves inside a bag for protection.
- ✦ Be aware of the people around you; don't be swayed by gossip.
- ✦ Take care of your body by bathing in cleansing essential oils.

Remember: The truth is that we are in this world to fulfill a purpose, even if we don't know it yet.

Yule

✦ ✦ ✦

Winter Solstice

December 20–21–22

The rebirth of the winter Sun

✦ ✦ ✦

At the icy heart of December, when the nights are longer and darkness reigns supreme, one of the brightest and most joyful festivals of the year ignites: Yule. It's an ancient celebration rooted in the tradition of Germanic peoples, which has survived across the centuries and still brings warmth and hope. Yule is a time when the light once again triumphs over darkness. The winter solstice, with its short days and deep nights, marks a stage with the smallest amount of sunlight, yet simultaneously represents the promise of new beginnings.

***The days will start to lengthen;
life will resume, and hope will blossom.***

Yule is a festival rich in European symbolism and traditions that have intertwined over time. The large bonfires, once central to the celebrations, nowadays are embodied by the candles lit in peoples' homes to light up the darkness and warm hearts. The Christmas log burning in the fireplace on Christmas Eve evokes the sacred stump that was set ablaze to favor fertility and rebirth. Yule, known in ancient times as *Jul*, undergoes a profound transformation with the advent of Christianity. Some of its traditions are assimilated into the Christmas celebrations by mixing ancient and modern. A testament to these links are pagan symbols such as the Christmas tree, which are still set up in people's homes today. This custom represents the peasant tradition of protecting life by welcoming an evergreen tree into one's home and thus becoming its guardians. Over time, this custom was absorbed into Catholic celebrations, giving rise to syncretism attesting to the persistence of ancient rituals and beliefs through the centuries.

Celebrating the frost

✦ ✦ ✦

YULE IS A TIME FOR SHARING AND JOY, a season for family and friends to gather and celebrate the return of the light, to honor one's ancestors, and to confidently look to the future. It is a celebration that goes beyond the spiritual; it is an opportunity to strengthen the earthly bonds with the people around us.

Just as during Samhain we honored the bond with our ancestors—blood of our blood—Yule celebrates our "community," the people with whom we share our daily lives. They are the ones we choose as travel companions, with whom we forge deep and mutual relationships.

At this time, we offer them gifts as symbols of gratitude for their presence in our lives.

We organize feasts to celebrate the time spent together, hoping that this bond will last for a long time to come. Yule is a time to contemplate nature, which in this period curtails its vitality in preparation for a rebirth. Everything around us settles down, taking on darker tones. The first snow starts to cover the coldest regions, an icy blanket that Mother Earth spreads to shelter future life. We humans also slow down our pace, and in these days we rediscover the value of "slow living." But how can we reinstate this natural rhythm in such a hectic world?

In our culture, the word "slow" often takes on negative connotations in association with laziness and low productivity. Yule asks us to refute this notion.

Slowing down does not equal missed opportunities; on the contrary, it enables us to appreciate the beauty of details that are often ignored. Sometimes, the most magical experiences are revealed through simple actions, like sipping herb tea in the presence of a cat.

Winter's breath

✦ ✦ ✦

THE MONTH'S ENERGY

This phase of the year is permeated by an atmosphere of anticipation and transformation. Everything seems to come to a standstill; some legends say that negative spirits roam the world on the coldest, most blustery days. These stories were intended to warn the young ones about the risks of winter; that is why the spells mainly focus on rituals to protect and develop one's personal power.

FULL MOON

The full Moon, influenced by the energy of the winter solstice above all, is a Moon that speaks to the awakening of personal power. At this time of the year, it is important to awaken one's energy and potential to counteract the energetic trend of the moment, which leads one to be more static.

During this phase, you can perform spells to attract good luck.

An ingredient connected to this phase of the year is the orange. Add some copper coins and an orange peel to a jar and expose it to the moonlight. This spell will help you attract abundance into your life.

NEW MOON

The new Moon that rises close to the winter solstice is a Moon that can be entrusted with the rituals of protection and banishment that are needed to ward off the heavy energies present at this specific time of year.

Make some protective charms by invoking help from the power of nature.

A plant especially connected to the traditions of this period is the holly. According to European folklore, its spiny leaves keep negative energies at bay. During the new Moon, expose a wreath of holly outside before placing it on your doorstep.

XII
THE HANGED MAN
XVIII
THE MOON

Conserving one's energy

✦ ✦ ✦

TO PREVENT WASTING ONE'S ENERGY, one must understand how it is misused, so as to intervene and rectify this cyclical nature that in the long run only causes harm. Answer these questions truthfully and instinctively.

✦ ***You find yourself in a complicated situation and resolve to invoke a spell to break your bond with something harmful. You focus on:***

A. The stress caused by your work; all those worries drain your energy.

B. Your fear of not being able to get the results you want; your expectations are exceedingly high.

✦ ***You are in the process of meditating. While you go to a safe place in your mind, you see before you:***

A. A silent forest covered in snow and a cozy fireplace to warm you up.

B. A beach with bright sand, the waves gently lapping against the shoreline.

✦ ***You have been granted a wish. What do you ask for?***

A. A lot of money so you can live well and even afford an easygoing life for your family members.

B. The true love from the people who choose to be at your side, even in the face of adversity.

✦ ***You are shuffling a tarot deck and select a card to visualize your problems. Before you appears:***

A. The Hanged Man. You feel coerced into a situation you're uncomfortable with, and you don't know how to get out of it.

B. The Moon. You realize that people around you are being insincere, and this causes you anguish.

✦ ***You resolve to follow the energy of the moment and start slowing down. Which situation do you find most challenging?***

A. Pacing yourself. You worry that people will think you are extremely lazy.

B. Needing to rest. You're afraid that if you stop, you won't be able to get started again.

YOU ANSWERED MOSTLY "A":
WHAT OTHERS THINK

To free oneself of the fear of judgment is to embrace one's own essence

✦ ✦ ✦

There is a monster lurking in the shadows, ready to crush our souls with its icy clutches—i.e., fear of other people's judgment. We act awkwardly and insecurely, trying to meet the expectations of those around us.

But who are these implacable judges? Imperfect people like us. Human beings in continuous evolution, who change their minds, make mistakes, and evolve over the course of their lives.

So why give them the power to define who we are? The truth is that no one will ever be completely satisfied with us. We are all different, with nuances that make us special; and precisely this uniqueness is our strength.

Recommended ritual: the ringing of bells.

YOU ANSWERED MOSTLY "B":
YOUR CONSTANT SELF-CRITICISM

To be understanding with oneself does not mean settling for mediocrity

✦ ✦ ✦

Do you ever feel an icy grip clutching at your chest? An inner voice scolding you relentlessly? If so, you know how being too hard on yourself feels. Of course, self-criticism can be a useful tool for improvement. It pushes you to give your best, to learn from your mistakes, and to grow as a person. Excessive self-criticism, though, turns into an implacable enemy that leads us into a vicious cycle of insecurity. Chasing perfection is akin to chasing an illusion. There is no such thing as a perfect human being, and trying to be one only exposes us to frustration and disappointment. True strength does not lie in rigor, but in kindness toward oneself. Learning to accept one's limitations, to forgive one's mistakes, and to recognize one's efforts, this is the key to real improvement.

Recommended ritual: the Yule log.

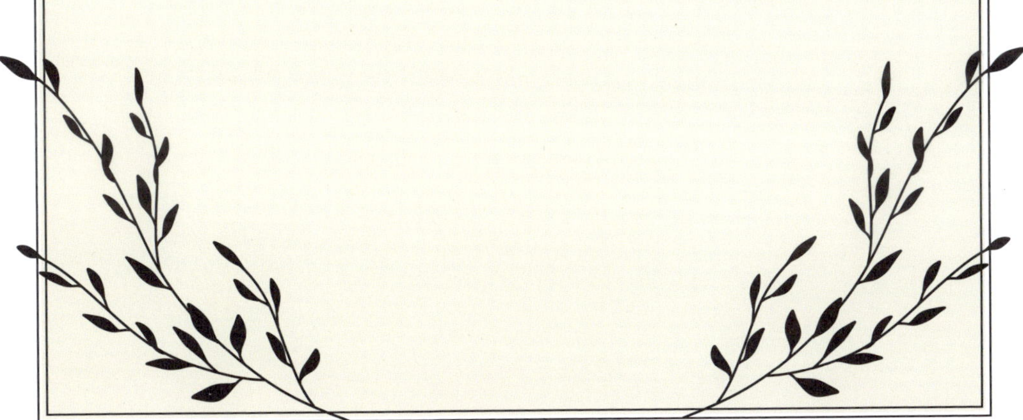

The return of magic

✦ ✦ ✦

Together, let's discover some rituals that can help us awaken the magic of this phase of the year.

CONNECTION: THE YULE LOG

Let's make a version of the Yule log to represent the return of the light that follows the darkness of winter, symbolizing the Sun's rebirth and the hopes for the new year.

SUPPLIES: Some fir sprigs, pinecones, dried orange slices, a jar, a tealight, a plate.

METHOD: To attract positive energy, use the plate to make a decorative holiday centerpiece that can also be used at family dinners. Place the jar with the candle inside it at the center of the plate and begin to decorate the space around it, alternating the fir sprigs used to depict the evergreen's resilience during the winter, and the pinecones, which represent fertility and are associated with the Great Mother, as well as the dried orange slices, the scent and color of which recall the Sun's energy. Enjoy crafting your decoration; and once it's completed, light the candle and use your spell to invoke these powers:

With this light that twinkles and shines,
I renew the bond that binds me to nature.
Its powers envelop and fill me,
the Sun and life bless my house.

Your Yule log is now ready; replace the candle in the jar as needed to keep the flame burning during the central days of the festival and throughout it, your connection to ancient customs.

PURIFICATION: THE RINGING OF BELLS

In European folklore, metal bells have the power to dispel negative energy and are a useful tool in our spells.

SUPPLIES: One or more metal bells, mint essential oil, a cinnamon stick, a dried sprig of rosemary, water.

METHOD: Before using your instrument, it is important to cleanse it carefully. For this reason, start by placing the bell under running water for a few minutes. As you do this, visualize the water's power removing any negativity from the object. Now, having carefully dried the bell, use a lighter to burn the cinnamon stick and the sprig of rosemary, spreading the smoke over the bell and visualizing how this process will remove any residues of negative energy inside the bell. Place a few drops of essential oil on your index finger and recite your spell to bless it:

Forged metal bell,
from today you shall be a magic instrument.
Your crystalline ring, which spreads through the air,
instantly dissolves negativity.

Rub oil onto the bell so that, from an everyday object, it turns into an officially magic tool that you can use to dispel any negative energy present by playing its melodious sound.

NATURE SPIRITS: THE GUARDIAN OF THE FOREST

Those who practice magic, in sync with the natural powers, recognize the incarnation of a sacred entity. It is believed that every natural site is inhabited by a guardian who takes care of the animals and spirits of that locale. Connecting with such powers is a way to obtain protection.

SUPPLIES: Dried fruit, apples, birdseed, a small jar of honey, a paper bag.

METHOD: Place all the ingredients inside the paper bag and, in daylight, go to a natural place away from people. It is important to choose a place where you feel comfortable and won't be interrupted during your practice. As you walk, scatter your offerings with the honey and focus on the energy around you.

With this simple, love-filled action, you will show your kindness to the nature spirits.

Once you have finished your offerings, humbly and respectfully introduce yourself to the place's guardian by reciting this short spell:

Ancestral Spirit, great and ancient guardian,
I offer you these gifts with a humble and grateful heart.
Watch over me, O mighty spirit;
in darkness and in light, may you always be present.

Try to ascertain your feelings. If your feelings are positive, your offerings have been accepted; if you feel ill at ease, stop and try again later.

The path from Yule to Imbolc

✦ ✦ ✦

To reach Imbolc starting from the energy of the winter solstice, we find ourselves facing the first month of the Gregorian calendar year: January.

In popular thinking, January is the month in which everything starts over; and with the new year, every wish becomes possible again. At this time, it is important not to carry the energy of the past with us, because we cannot renew ourselves if we remain anchored to the way we were.

If we wish for something new, first we must shift our mind's reality.

The zodiac sign that teaches us how to deal with this detachment is Capricorn, which is represented by a goat with a fish tail. This symbol reminds us that in order to really let go of the past, we must do so in a carefree manner and with peace of mind. Working on these feelings is key to getting our new year's journey off to a good start.

At this stage, the main theme is: Above all, to change your life you must be ready for change.

How to put such transformation into practice:

- ✦ Remove all the objects that you no longer need, or which exude negative energy, from your home.
- ✦ Take the time to read and widen your knowledge.
- ✦ When faced with an obstacle, do not react impulsively: regain your mental acuity by focusing on your breath for a few seconds.
- ✦ Face life's problems one at a time; consider what strategy to put in place.
- ✦ Be generous: if you see someone struggling, help them without seeking anything in return.
- ✦ If your mind keeps dwelling on the past, divert your attention; don't give in to your thoughts.

Remember: If something in your past persists, it is because it is unworthy of being part of your future.

Imbolc

✦ ✦ ✦

CANDLEMAS

JANUARY 31—FEBRUARY 1–2

To be reborn, I let go

✦ ✦ ✦

TRAVERSING THE LONG SNOWY PATH, we come across a clearing tentatively brightened by the Sun; the rays melt the white mantle from which they rise, the princes of February, the snowdrops.

This is Imbolc's entry into the Wheel of the Year, during the icy heart of winter.

Imbolc represents a pause, with its transitory position between winter's darkness and spring's first warm glow.

Theories abound over the true origin of the festival's name; the most cited is ***Imbolg***, which in Old Gaelic means "inside the womb."

This name refers to the energy that at this time of year lies dormant in the womb of Mother Earth, peeping through from time to time.

We are asked to experience its energy calmly and quietly, because the beauty of things is revealed while we wait.

Imbolc, often associated with the lore of Candlemas or Oimelc, is tasked with removing and awakening people's spirituality; it foreshadows the restoration of life and is the harbinger of the Sun's return.

Oimelc, which means "sheep's milk," is rooted in peasant tradition; the milk produced by the flock will also be used to feed the community and, as such, is important enough to warrant a celebration.

Candlemas, a name commonly used for the Catholic festival on February 2, is linked to Ancient Roman customs of purification.

In neopaganism, the magic of the sabbat evokes these traditions by including the following into the celebrations: the blessing of the candles that will be used throughout the year; the turning on of lights to symbolize the Sun's slow awakening; and cleansing rituals.

Sacrifice and purification

✦ ✦ ✦

WITH IMBOLC, THE FEEBLE SUN SLOWLY REVEALS ITSELF WHILE THE STILL EARTH stirs beneath the icy ground. Nature's impulse is to awaken from winter's slumber, yet it does so with the slow, silent pace of a seed developing its roots.

This sabbat's energy is mostly introspective. It is not a sudden explosion, but rather a slow crescendo, a whisper becoming louder and louder.

Despite its impetus for rebirth, in this phase nature still bears the austere aspect of winter. It might be bitter cold, the wind icy, and the fields still covered in snow, but none of it can stop the eternal cycle of transformation.

The approach of February was a time to rejoice at having survived the winter, which required considerable effort and deprivation.

Despite the challenges, at this time people readied themselves for the farm-work ahead that would ensure their survival in the following months and, for this reason, the festival overlaps with peasant customs and folklore.

To ensure that such a massive effort would reap its rewards, at this time it was important to dispel any kind of negativity, which is why water plays such an important role.

Due to its endless flow, in the collective imagination it symbolizes a powerful cycle capable of cleansing and delivering people of stagnant, negative energy weighing them down.

Its power is also linked to the emotions. Just like a mermaid explores the depths of the sea in search of sunken treasure, water seeps into the abyss of our being, dissolving blockages and bringing our most precious and pure feelings to the surface.

Independent thinking

✦ ✦ ✦

THE MONTH'S ENERGY

February is associated with Aquarius, a zodiac sign characterized by independence and vision. The power of this sign guides us to understand the importance of acting according to our values, without needing to conform to conventional standards. This message mirrors Imbolc's influence, given that we are in a defining phase of our identity, just as nature is slowly coming back to life.

FULL MOON

The second month of the year sees the lunar energy manifest itself in an introspective and immaterial way. We must firmly hold on to our ideas and focus on realizing our dreams, which epitomize the spark of our desires.

During this phase, focus on working with the magic of dreams to foster their realization.

Creating a charm to support your dreams is simple: just combine three tablespoons of dried chamomile and an amethyst. Charge it with lunar energy overnight and place it next to your bed, it will encourage sleep and help you realize your wishes.

NEW MOON

During this month of purification, we use energy to attract strength into our lives, devoting ourselves to cleansing our magic instruments such as crystals and fortune-telling tools.

During the new Moon, bless some ingredients you will use in cleansing rituals.

To make an infusion, place some garlic peel in a jar of oil and leave it the whole night to absorb the Moon's energy. You can use a few drops of this oil on a cloth to clean and purify objects energetically, taking care to avoid contact with delicate surfaces and the skin.

The connection of the spirit

✦ ✦ ✦

When we are in a phase of rebirth, nature teaches us the importance of understanding our connection with past and future energies. Concentrate and answer the questions by selecting what most resonates with your soul.

✦ ***Many people are fascinated by magic. In your opinion, what does following this path entail?***

A. It is immersing oneself into a world rich in wisdom, in which ancient traditions can be rediscovered.

B. To change one's life by learning about energy through study and commitment.

✦ ***You need to create a garden, and you can choose the plants in the certainty that they will thrive. Which ones do you opt for?***

A. Medicinal and aromatic herbs that can be used in infusions.

B. Exotic plants and flowers with bright colors and intoxicating scents.

✦ ***In time, those who work with magic often create their own book of shadows, a tome in which to record spells and notes of their studies. How do you imagine yours?***

A. A large journal, bound in leather with some engraved and finely painted signets.

B. A book with a colorful cover, filled with hand-decorated pages.

✦ ***You need to make a spell for protection, so you decide to cast a spell on a jewel that you can wear every day. What do you use?***

A. A necklace with dark-colored stones that encapsulate mystery and elegance.

B. A necklace made of metal pendants, shells, and wooden beads.

✦ ***You are crossing a path in a snowy place. You reach a crossroads. Which way do you choose?***

A. Along a path with smooth stones that, by looking carefully, you realize leads to a medieval village where you can find comfortable lodgings.

B. A paved path leading to a well-lit restaurant. You will certainly be able to eat a hot, invigorating meal here.

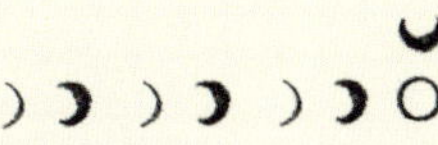

YOU ANSWERED MOSTLY "A":
THE WISDOM OF THE PAST

Immersing oneself in the past does not mean giving up on the future, but building on solid foundations

✦ ✦ ✦

The experiences of those who came before us teach us not to repeat the same mistakes, to value our successes, and to confidently look at new challenges. Connecting to the past allows us to rediscover our roots, to understand our identity. It is a journey of knowledge and personal growth, because it is through our family's history or that of ancient peoples that we can gain great wisdom, though one must remember not to be tied down by the past. We cannot live forever amongst memories: we need to propel ourselves into the future with courage and determination. The energy of the past gives us stability and knowledge, though it is our present actions that determine our destiny.

Recommended ritual: let it flow.

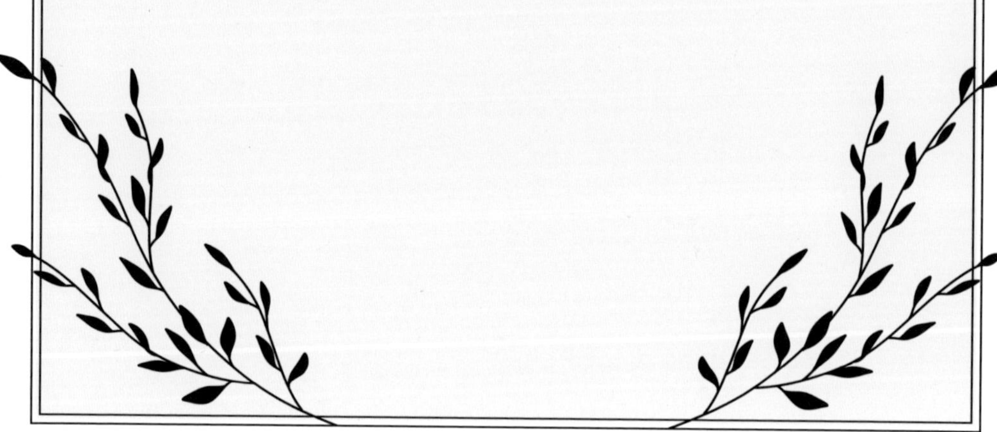

YOU ANSWERED MOSTLY "B":
A VISION OF THE FUTURE

The future is a blank canvas to be painted with the colors of our dreams

✦ ✦ ✦

Dreaming about the future is not the same as escaping reality; rather, it is about expanding the boundaries of what is possible and shaping the world we want. The future is not a predetermined place, but an opportunity to let go of current limitations and fly toward boundless horizons, where anything is possible. The future is an opportunity to make an indelible mark on the world; it's up to us to decide what kind of mark this will be, and what it will bring to the world. The key is to always keep in mind that, in order to create what is to come, we must act today, as our actions shape our destiny. Every thought, every word is energy, so carefully choose what energies will nourish and define tomorrow's version of you.

Recommended ritual: the impenetrable wall of ice.

The magic of transformation

✦ ✦ ✦

The magic practices related to Imbolc are many, and generally they recall the powers of water and fire. Together, let's rediscover these magnificent rituals that will accompany us on our journey through the Wheel of the Year.

CONNECTION: THE SPIRIT OF FIRE

Fire is a dynamic and ever-changing element that takes on great importance in many different traditions. We channel Imbolc's energy to attract its spirit into your home.

SUPPLIES: A large candle, four tea lights, matches, cinnamon essential oil, a compass.

METHOD: Place the large candle at the center of a table and, with the help of the compass, identify the four cardinal points around it. Take care to accurately identify the north, then place a tea light at each point: north, south, east, and west. Rub a few drops of oil on the lower part of the large candle and, taking great care, mimic the transfer of the fire's power: first, light the large candle; then, using the matches, deliver its flame to the tea lights, which you will allow to burn out completely. Perform this process by starting from the north and moving clockwise to attract energy.

As you do this, say:

From the north, from the east, from the south, from the west,
fire spirit, your attention I request.
I invite and welcome you to this place,
through this candle come to my aid.

Once you are finished, your candle is blessed and can be reused in other rituals to conjure the fire spirit's magic in your aid.

PURIFICATION: LETTING FLOW

Water is a purifying element that simultaneously lets us get in touch with our emotions. Carry out this ritual bath to connect to its power.

SUPPLIES: A bowl of water, rose petals, rice grains, lavender essential oil, three tablespoons of sea salt.

METHOD: Place all the ingredients in the bowl of water, and stir three times counterclockwise. The water should become infused with pleasing scents that release its magic.

Now place your palms in contact with the water and cast a spell over it by saying:

Without fear I explore the abyss of my soul.
I now release all feelings
that prevent me from living freely.

Wait a few moments by keeping your eyes closed and listening to your heart. Delve into your feelings, what is causing you pain? What prevents you from facing your life freely?

Feel these emotions flowing from your body, through your hands and into the water, as if they no longer belonged to you.

At this stage, proceed calmly without holding back your emotions; let your tears flow if you feel the need to cry.

Once this process is completed, thank the universe for the gift it has given you, then go outside and throw out the water.

By discarding the water, you are releasing your negative emotions into the arms of the universe.

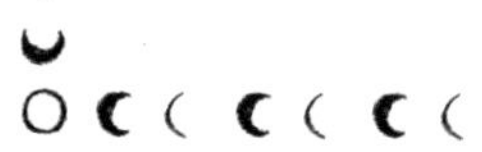

PROTECTION: THE IMPASSABLE WALL OF ICE

Snow is an element that is much used in the magic practices of Northern Europe folklore. Its purity and chill are associated with the power to stave off what may cause us harm. Nowadays, as finding snow can be challenging, ice offers a valid substitute.

SUPPLIES: A glass, ice, a sheet of paper, a felt pen.

METHOD: Use the felt pen to write what you seek protection from on the sheet of paper: it could be someone at work causing you stress or some challenging situations making you uncomfortable; alternatively, if you are unsure how to clearly state your purpose, simply write down the words "negative energy."

Fill the jar with ice and gently fold the paper. Put the paper inside the jar, trying to place it in the middle: ideally, the paper should be surrounded by ice cubes.

Now recite the spell:

Water transformed into pure ice,
drive away what is dark from my path.
Now protected from evil,
my spirit I can set free.

Allow the ice to slowly melt. Once this step is completed, without touching it directly, check the paper to see if what you wrote has become illegible. If it is still legible, you must repeat the ritual; if it is illegible, the spell has worked and you can throw out the water.

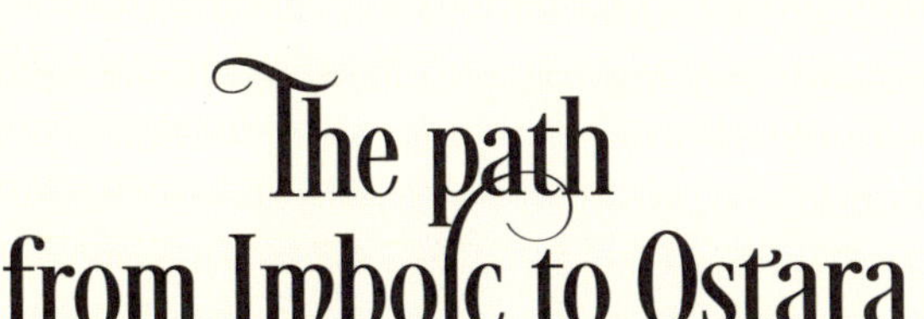

The path from Imbolc to Ostara

✦ ✦ ✦

During this transitional moment, the energy remains sluggish and focused on inactivity: it is an opportunity to slow down, save one's strength, and meditate. In a fast-paced world, where everything needs to be done quickly, this month provides an opportunity to rediscover the value of stillness and one's inner rhythm.

Listening to one's body and soul is fundamental. We must take our time to rest, recharge our batteries, and reconnect to our inner selves.

Let us remember that waiting is not a waste of time, but a valuable opportunity to grow and prepare for new challenges.

Let's not become anxious: let's practice listening to our bodies; and let's do what feels positive, without rushing or stress.

The main theme of this phase is finding our inner rhythm, as this is the only way to fully experience the reawakening of power.

To fully embrace this energy, here's what you can do:

- ✦ Creativity: expressing yourself creatively is a great way to release stress and negative emotions.
- ✦ A digital detox day: choose one day a week to forgo mobile phones, computers, and social media.
- ✦ Mindful breathing: take a few minutes to focus on your breathing. It can help you calm your mind and reduce stress.
- ✦ Quality sleep: institute a relaxing evening routine before bed.
- ✦ Music: listen to music that relaxes you or makes you feel good.
- ✦ Reading: take time to read a book you are passionate about or that inspires you.
- ✦ A relaxing bath: take a warm bath with essential oils to unwind your body and mind.

Remember: slowness does not equate to laziness, but rather to awareness and self-respect.

✦ ✦ ✦

SPRING EQUINOX

MARCH 20–21–22

The rebirth of the true self

✦ ✦ ✦

In the Northern Hemisphere, the spring equinox occurs in March, a month characterized by effervescent and chaotic energy. At this time, everything seems to change at a surprising pace.

The days whirl, alternating storms and sunshine; the trees clad in their best buds suddenly explode, bringing color into the world.

The animals, awakening from their slumber, reconquer the forests, the skies, and the countryside.

The equinox is the time of year when the battle between light and darkness resolves in balance. The two forces are in stasis; on this day neither rival prevails over the other.

And, on this exact occasion, everlasting magic takes place: Mother Nature calls to us, and her charm is so potent that it even shakes the souls of those who are still asleep.

Wake up and fight; you need to be reborn.
You are stuck at a crossroads, and you must take your first step.
This is the moment to choose who you want to become.

In the past, the awakening of the Earth constituted a significant event, since the fate of the harvest was key to the survival of entire villages.

That is why we still celebrate propitiatory rituals handed down through the centuries that aim to both attract abundance and dispel the old year's energy.

In various places around the world, spring cleaning is carried out inside the home, a magical task, in which all rooms are cleansed and reorganized physically and energetically.

Ostara is the best time for new beginnings: just like a guest wipes their shoes before entering the house, we are called to lighten ourselves of the "dirt" of negativity prior to entering this new phase of our lives.

With strong roots it is time to bloom

✦ ✦ ✦

THE WHEEL OF THE YEAR PHASE that marks the arrival of the spring equinox coincides with the magic of reawakening to life and the mystery of rebirth.

The word Ostara originates from the Anglo-Saxon name of the goddess Eostre; however, according to alternative theories from the Indo-European root, it derives from the term ***to shine*** or ***dawn***. It is believed that this lore predates Easter and that its archaic rituals relating to the Earth, the harvest, and fairy spirits recall its essence by immersing us in the flow of magic energy that honors the return of life and abundance.

Energetically, this festival comes along at the beginning of the natural realm's transformation. The birds in the sky sing frantically as they prepare the nests in which they will raise their offspring; in the meadows, the cubs are suckled. Everything changes and every day seems different from the one before.

The magic of metamorphosis is all around us and in our every breath.

At the end of winter, human beings are driven toward freedom. They are called to move gently within the flow of transmutation, in search of balance, given that in this balance they will find their strength.

Nowadays, we still come across traditions handed down from the past that honor this cosmic event with the use of ancient symbols: painted eggs, which are also used in the Catholic Easter; statues of hares, messengers of abundance and fertility in European folklore; daffodils and buds symbolizing victory and new beginnings, in the language of flowers.

On a magical level, Ostara represents the spirit balanced between dynamism and inaction. On one hand there is a desire to expand toward the sky; on the other there is the tentative warmth of a power needing time to awaken.

Balance and introspection

✦ ✦ ✦

THE MONTH'S ENERGY

The end of March and the beginning of April represent the point at which the power of each element around us is tangible. The gentle rain, the tentative Sun, the light breeze, and the blooming Earth tell us that we are part of a whole and our task is to seek out the beauty within and without ourselves.

At this time of year, we are often likely to feel dynamic and creative, and simultaneously distracted and confused. Our task is to act calmly and focus our energy on achieving our future goals.

FULL MOON

The full Moon tinged with the magic of the equinox represents the blooming season. It is fueled by the power of change, which makes it especially chaotic and mutable. In the chaos of this lunar phase, we can tap into the creative powers to shape reality to our advantage.

During this magical moment,
you can boost your spiritual equilibrium.

Use two candles, one white and one black, representing your strengths and weaknesses; burning them both in this lunar phase will assist you by nurturing your constructive self and lessening your destructive self.

NEW MOON

Within a short period of time, the Moon goes from totally losing its light to regaining the vigor to shine again. Likewise, we are led to sink into the darkest part of our soul, only to rise again with renewed ardor.

During this lunar phase, devote yourself to cleansing your soul.

Clear quartz is a valuable ally for this task; charge it with energy by placing it outside and exposing it to the new Moon, then place it under your pillow. Its properties will help you disperse any pent-up negativity.

I am the seed. What will help me blossom?

Philosopher Sir Francis Bacon is said to have coined the phrase "Knowledge is power," a concept that also applies to our spiritual path. It is fundamental to connect with our magic, as it supports us in understanding who we are and what we need.

Concentrate and answer the questions that most resonate with your soul.

✦ ***You're walking through an art gallery. Before you are several landscape paintings. Which one is most in tune with your state of mind?***

A. A lake with light shining across the light ripples.
B. A night garden lit by a lantern.

✦ ***It is a loved one's birthday and you decide to get a flower arrangement from a florist to bring as a gift. Which flowers do you choose?***

A. White roses, lavender, and white verbena.
B. Marigolds, red gerberas, and tulips.

✦ ***You are walking through a lush forest. By following a path, you realize you have reached a clearing. Before you there is:***

A. A crystal-clear stream with water flowing and gushing between the rocks.
B. A village celebration with cheerful music, people dancing and having fun.

✦ ***While meditating, you decide to ask a spirit animal to come to your aid. You wait; then the following appears before you:***

A. A wise old turtle swimming around you.
B. A spirited and fancy-free butterfly inviting you to walk through the flowers.

✦ ***In the window display of an esoteric shop, you see some interesting objects, so you decide to go inside and browse. You are greeted by the scent of incense. You then see some magical tools before you. Which one attracts you the most?***

A. A large cast-iron cauldron engraved with symbols.
B. An oak-wood wand set with semi-precious stones.

YOU ANSWERED MOSTLY "A":
CLEANSE YOUR ESSENCE

Let go of what weighs you down and take flight

✦ ✦ ✦

Living in modern society can be tiring and, over time, this feeling of heaviness can erode your personal power by slowly depleting it.

Lack of energy can feel like being stuck in an endless loop, even though you are not.

You can exit this vicious circle by starting to devote time to self-care for the mind and body. What is key is to practice identifying what boosts your personal power and what causes negative feelings. We often don't realize how much negativity we absorb through social interactions in the outside world, which is why it's important to disencumber one's energy and begin listening to our inner selves.

There are many ways to heal and, if you need to, to seek help.

Recommended ritual: the wisdom of the snake.

YOU ANSWERED MOSTLY "B":
EXPAND YOUR POWER

It's time to nurture your true essence

✦ ✦ ✦

We always have time for everything, yet we never have enough for ourselves. Although our to-do list is very long, it does not foresee even a small time slot for ourselves; thus, our power is slowly depleted. Who will take care of you? Who will allow you to regain that strength? You.

It's important to understand that to operate at our best, our routine needs to include practices that increase our personal power. Like a valuable plant that requires water and care, you too must make time to nurture your soul and power by starting to shift your mindset: you are as important as everything else in your life: you just have to believe it.

Recommended rituals: sowing a wish.

I allow energy to bloom

✦ ✦ ✦

With the spring equinox, we rediscover the rituals inspired by the tradition of celebrating life that used to take place during these days.

CELEBRATION: THE LADY OF SPRING AND FATE

In European tales and folklore, spring is often depicted as a female deity dancing in the meadows and woods, changing everything with her magic touch. Through this ritual we evoke the symbolism connected to Ostara.

SUPPLIES: Myrrh incense, a cloth bag, a candle, textile paints, dried flowers.

METHOD: After spreading the incense smoke through the room in which you are performing the ritual, place the candle and the cloth bag before you.

Focus and let yourself be carried away by the creative energy around you, then draw the silhouette of a female figure on the fabric. As you use your colors, visualize the wonder of spring, its colors and scents; this way the bag will be charged by these energies. Express yourself and enjoy this process: you are bringing your charm to life. Add the dried flowers to the bag and, once you have finished your creation, recite the following words while looking at the candle's flame:

Lady of spring and of the eternal life cycle,
like the flowers that you make bloom,
may this charm attract good luck.

Wait for the color to dry, then store your charm in a safe place so that no one can touch it.

REBIRTH: THE WISDOM OF THE SNAKE

In primitive lore, the snake symbolized the ancestral power of metamorphosis that is needed for our evolution. We work with this ancient icon to awaken the powers of renewal in our lives.

SUPPLIES: A natural wax candle, matches, an engraving tool (such as a toothpick).

METHOD: Start by preparing the candle by charging it with your purpose; do this by using the toothpick to carve the shape of a snake with the head positioned toward the wick and the tail toward the base of the candle.

Let your creativity run wild while you draw.

As you create the design, focus on the energy conjured by your actions. Visualize the snake shedding its old skin and being reborn. As you engrave, you are summoning its power and likewise preparing to shed what no longer serves you, in order to become stronger.

Maintain your focus and proceed to carve a few letters or symbols that evoke what you want to let go of. They can be simple drawings or the initials of key words.

As you do this, say:

Now I sculpt, now I let go,
every energy away from me will go
once the flame has consumed them.

Light the candle and let it burn out completely. During this process, keep an eye on the flame as it slowly dissolves any obstacles.

ABUNDANCE: SOWING A WISH

To attract abundance into our home, we use the symbol of the egg.

Carrying within the seed of life, it represents birth, fertility, and procreation. Its hatching is considered an epiphany, and we shall conjure such powers.

SUPPLIES: A fresh egg or an oval-shaped earthenware container, basil seeds, soil, a needle, a teaspoon.

METHOD: Very gently, make a hole in the upper part of the egg. Choose the thinnest part. Slowly enlarge it and then empty the egg, taking care not to damage the shell.

Use a teaspoon to place a portion of the soil into the empty eggshell (or the container).

Hold the seeds firmly in your hands and warm them with your body heat. Focus on your wishes. Visualize them inside the seeds. They must be concrete images, visions of your life as if they were already fulfilled. As you delineate your intent, whisper:

Seeds of life, guardians of my will,
welcome my dream, make it flourish.
Now what I desire is already real.

Now gently place the seeds in the shell, or container, and cover them with a bit of soil.

You will then have to take care of your spell by regularly watering the soil and watching over the growth process. If life blossoms from the seeds, your wishes will soon come true.

The path from Ostara to Beltane

✦ ✦ ✦

THE TRANSITIONAL PERIOD between the spring equinox and the festival of Beltane is characterized by an increase in energy toward ongoing change. During the spring equinox, the miracle of life allows the eggs to hatch. At this phase of growth, the chicks will be fed and strengthened so they can survive on their own.

Nature guides us and teaches us that to be free, we must grow and empower ourselves.

We set out on this path starting with the creative sign of Pisces, then traversing the fiery lands of ambitious Aries. Likewise, our personal transformation will change from a more introspective phase to a more dynamic one. With constant effort, change will embrace every aspect of life.

This is a propitious time to strengthen our power, since it is the magic of movement that allows things to transform and evolve.

The main theme of this phase is:
Let's learn to nurture ourselves before nurturing the world.
At this time, you must heal yourself and your spirit.

To truly experience this energy, here are some practical tips that will help you to bring about change:

- ✦ To attract good luck, start the day with positive thoughts.
- ✦ Tidy your home to conjure new energy into your life.
- ✦ Take care of others, especially defenseless animals.
- ✦ Begin writing in your magic journal, noting your progress.
- ✦ Foster the love for what makes you unique; value your gifts.
- ✦ Your studies should include getting to know a divination method.
- ✦ Rest to ground your personal power.

Remember: your power is your engine and every day is an opportunity to enhance your magic.

Beltane

✦ ✦ ✦

MAY DAY

APRIL 31–MAY 1–2

The fire and the impetus of the wild spirit

✦ ✦ ✦

THE FESTIVAL OF BELTANE represents the point at which the energy of rebirth and transformation reach their ultimate expression. The origin of the term in Old Irish is believed to mean "bright fire."

It takes place in the month of May, which occurs during the stability of Taurus and matures under the dynamic sign of Gemini. This duality signifies the sacred union between masculine and feminine powers, which, in the indomitable chaos of love, generates life.

A vortex of magic envelops reality: witches dance in the fields astride their brooms, sacred fires burn like beacons warding off evil, and symbols of fertility are at the center of songs and dances.

Such imagery reveals the secrets of this celebration, which is connected to fire's energetic power and Earth's sacredness.

The first symbol utilized is the maypole. Consisting of a pole in the ground, it signifies the divine marriage between heaven and Earth and the union between male and female. In centuries past, it was customary to dance around the maypole creating geometric shapes like the circle and the spiral, to conjure the eternal energy cycle.

The second symbol of these traditions is the bonfire. In the folklore of some European countries, the fire was situated at the center of the celebrations, during which tests of courage, rituals to ward off evil, and love spells took place.

During such celebrations, the fire is considered sacred. The ash is collected and scattered over the fields to fertilize the soil and restore the energy channeled during the festival.

This type of conciliatory ritual embodies the sacred link between humans and the Earth. The peasants, who are deeply attached to it, are its custodians.

I courageously outline my path

✦ ✦ ✦

When the Wheel of the Year reaches Beltane, our spirit has traveled a long way, leading us to abandon the "dark semester," the phase of the year in which the Sun's power fades and darkness triumphs.

This festival invites us to celebrate all the efforts that make life precious, due to its complexity. This is a time to connect with nature, an opportunity to rejoice, to love, to transform and expand; finally, the seed of consciousness has developed within us, simply by facing our daily challenges without losing heart. We are now ready to embrace the infinite potential that resides within us.

Energetically, in this phase of life, a person feels an irresistible "outward" thrust. Just like a nestling is ready to take flight, instinctively trusting its wings, a person is ready to conquer the outside world in a fanciful rite of passage toward maturity.

Every individual is called upon to bravely leave their comfort zone.

In pursuit of this call and starting with the month of May, the games and skill tests of village festivals in various European countries were seen by young people as an opportunity to demonstrate their abilities and prowess. Through such contests, they not only challenged themselves physically and mentally, but they also established strong brotherly bonds.

On a magical level, this mystical power favors the transfer of energy from the incorporeal state of spirit to the corporeal state of matter.

What until yesterday was just a dream now seems close: within us, we perceive the power to manifest what is deeply rooted in our hearts.

Creation and renewal

✦ ✦ ✦

THE MONTH'S ENERGY

May teaches us that transformation is an integral part of our daily lives and that sameness is merely an illusion. During the transition between spring and summer, nature undergoes a significant transformation, in which the flowers of farmed plants turn into fruit or vegetables. This is a phase for consolidating power: what before was the unreal world of our desires now has a chance to materialize; thus, it is fundamental to act in a way that facilitates all this.

FULL MOON

This month's full Moon arrives with the strength required to increase and consolidate one's personal power and connection to nature. Therefore, during this phase, you will have the opportunity to make this valuable experience.

By exploiting its creative magic, you can create a ritual to manifest your desires.

A natural element you can use is laurel, which in the language of flowers symbolizes victory. In a bag, put five leaves on which you will have written your wish by evenly separating the words. Keep this charm in a safe place.

NEW MOON

This month's new Moon brings with it a creative spark and teaches us that a good start is half the battle; therefore, be sure to let go of what's holding you back.

Under its influence, focus on cleansing practices in your home.

Let's use a white candle with which we can channel the fire's power. Place it on a fireproof plate and sprinkle a handful of rock salt around the base of the candle. Let it burn out while keeping an eye on the flame. This will eliminate negative energy.

What energy do I conceal in my soul?

✦ ✦ ✦

In order to define ourselves, we need to know and understand what we really need. If we understand our needs, we can discover ourselves without preconceptions and without idealizing ourselves.

Concentrate and answer the questions that most resonate with your soul.

✦ ***Visualize yourself before a giant fire. You hold some gifts in your hands that you will commit to the flames in exchange for good luck. What are your offerings?***

A. An item from your past that you want to get rid of.

B. A valuable family jewel you inherited.

✦ ***You are invited to a mystery ball. You don't know what the theme is. But by closely inspecting the envelope's decorations and the embossed calligraphy, you immediately gather the event's significance. What outfit do you choose for the occasion?***

A. You rely on an outfit that shows off your sensuality and strong points.

B. You go for a classic, elegant outfit in dark colors.

✦ ***Through an old mirror, you discover that you have the ability to see your own personal power. What is revealed takes on the appearance of a gemstone. In what form do you visualize the energy around you?***

A. Like the drops of a precious ruby.

B. A square-cut emerald.

✦ ***You are commissioned to create an artwork that represents your vision of the world. You can choose which technique to use. Following your inspiration, you begin to create:***

A. A musical piece in which you utilize the notes to convey the impetus of your life force.

B. A statue, shaping the material to depict what you consider to be true beauty.

✦ ***The ideal house in which to spend a relaxing weekend is:***

A. In the countryside; a house with a swimming pool where you can sunbathe and relax.

B. A silent and peaceful mountain house, situated in the green heart of a forest.

YOU ANSWERED MOSTLY "A":
ENERGY OF PASSION AND COURAGE

The sacred flame of courage burns in the depths of your soul

✦ ✦ ✦

It is a powerful spark, pushing you beyond your fears and leading you to make bold choices and to be able to manifest your dreams; however, to feed it you need a fundamental ingredient: self-love.

Self-love does not imply being selfish or vain. It means accepting oneself completely, with one's strengths and weaknesses, without judgment. It means taking care of oneself, one's body and mind, nurturing one's dreams and persevering in the face of obstacles and challenges. Self-love is a journey, not a destination. There will be difficult times; but when you feel frozen by fear or insecurity, remember that the power is already inside you.

Ignite your flame and let it guide you toward your amazing new life.

Recommended ritual: the spell of cutting.

YOU ANSWERED MOSTLY "B":
THE ENERGY OF TENACITY AND CREATION

Inside you beats a deep-rooted power, like the fertile Earth

✦ ✦ ✦

It represents your tenacity, your connection to your roots and your predisposition to create solid projects; however, don't forget that just as the Earth requires nourishment, your talents also require nurturing in a committed and patient manner.

Just like the tree's deep roots allow it to withstand the storm, you too must feed your strength with serenity.

Serenity is not the absence of problems or challenges, but rather the ability to face them calmly, lucidly, and resiliently. It is a way of living in the present without being overwhelmed by fears or negative thoughts.

Never forget the importance of nurturing and protecting your energy.

Recommended ritual: the intertwining of desires.

The dance between light and shadow

✦ ✦ ✦

In this practical chapter we will look at how to live and experiment with Beltane's power. To put spells into practice and celebrate this beautiful holiday, let yourself be carried away by the newly discovered symbols and forces.

FORTUNE: THE INTERTWINING OF DESIRES

Beltane is a festival characterized by very powerful positive energies, which is why we will attract luck into our lives by channeling them through this simple ritual.

SUPPLIES: wildflowers; two red candles; two pendants depicting lucky symbols such as a four-leaf clover or a small acorn; colored ribbons in natural cotton.

METHOD: in a meditative atmosphere, decorate the space in which you will cast the spell by lighting the candles. Breathe deeply to center yourself. Ground yourself by imagining a golden flame blazing inside your chest. Without losing your concentration, start braiding the flowers and ribbons, making a precious charm; with each knot and movement, imprint your mind's energy into the material world. As you do this, visualize your new life in every detail: your appearance, your home, your job.

Think big; don't be afraid; dare to dream with passion. Before finishing the braid, place one of the pendants at each end of the charm. In your mind, say the following words:

With this charm I define my desire
until the last knot is tied.
Now my future has already changed.

Place the charm in a safe place and keep it until the next Beltane.

PURIFICATION: THE SPELL OF CUTTING

Scissors universally symbolize rupture; in this cleansing ritual, they become the main tool to free yourself of negativity.

SUPPLIES: A new pair of scissors (must be unused), a sheet of paper, a pen, a small fireproof container, matches.

METHOD: In a quiet place where you can work uninterrupted, take a sheet of paper and write down all negative, limiting thoughts or fears that you want to eliminate from your life. Hold the sheet of paper in one hand and the scissors in the other. Visualize the scissors cutting the negative energy represented by your words. Firmly cut the sheet of paper into small pieces. Gather the fragments into the fireproof container and light them carefully. Make sure they are completely burned and the ash is fully extinguished before continuing. Take great care during this stage.

As you watch the flames burn, recite the following spell:

With the power of these scissors and fire,
I cut away negativity, I transform.
I make room for light and positivity in my life.

Once the ash is completely extinguished, you can scatter it in the wild or bury it in a safe place. Thoroughly clean the scissors and, from now on, use them exclusively for positive purposes as a symbol of renewal and transformation.

NATURAL ENERGY: THE SPIRIT OF THE HOUSE

During this phase, the veil between the physical and spiritual worlds is thin. This makes it easier to communicate with spirits and ancestors. According to the folklore in some European countries, every house has a spirit that lives inside it and protects it. Forging a good relationship with this small entity is fundamental when you demand protection and good luck in exchange of gifts.

SUPPLIES: A piece of bread, a teaspoon of honey or jam, a small wildflower, a handkerchief in natural fibers.

METHOD: Somewhere in your home, place the bread, the honey, and the flower on the handkerchief. Select the place carefully, as it should not be accessible to pets, other people, and ants. Close your eyes and connect to your home's energy; visualize it in your mind and say the following spell:

Guardian spirit of this home,
I offer you these gifts as a sign of friendship.
I ask you to protect my home
and to bring luck and prosperity into my life.

Leave the offerings on the handkerchief for one day and one night.

The following day, dispose of the gifts outdoors.

Place the handkerchief in a special place in your home. It will be a link between you and your "imp."

Regularly nurture your relationship with your new friend with gifts such as sweets, coffee, bread, flowers, and fruit.

The path from Beltane to Litha

✦ ✦ ✦

THE PERIOD BETWEEN BELTANE AND LITHA is characterized by a dynamic and transformative energy full of contradictions and excitement. At this time of year, the Sun in the Northern Hemisphere reaches its maximum intensity, in a growing cycle that conveys the importance of the Sun's light and power.

This transitory phase occurs mainly when the Sun's energy is in the air sign of Gemini.

Gemini is a sign ruled by Mercury and has a lively and inquisitive intellectual energy that promotes learning and communication, and adapts to new situations. It is a favorable time to reassess oneself, to let go of old habits, to embrace new projects, and to establish new connections with others.

The main theme of this phase is:
the enjoyment of life and nurturing one's spirit with positive energy.
This is the point when you give yourself time to do what you love.

To thoroughly embrace this energy and prepare for Litha's arrival, here's what you can do:

- ✦ Read books and articles or watch documentaries on topics that intrigue you.
- ✦ Take part in conversations and talks about topics you are passionate about.
- ✦ Create a social environment in which you can share your enthusiasm.
- ✦ Travel somewhere new and appreciate its energy.
- ✦ Volunteer or take part in charitable activities in your community.
- ✦ Feed your creative spirit by writing, painting, or drawing. Choose what best represents you.
- ✦ Work with natural energies and connect with the nature spirits living around you.

Remember: There is no right or wrong way to embrace this energy. Experiment with different activities, find those that make you feel most alive, nurture your connection with the whole.

Litha

✦ ✦ ✦

SUMMER SOLSTICE

JUNE 20–21–22

Celebrating abundance

✦ ✦ ✦

Since Neolithic times, human beings have celebrated the solstice, an astronomical phenomenon in which the Sun in the Northern Hemisphere reaches its zenith, marking the beginning of a new season, summer. This anniversary takes on a deep symbolic and spiritual meaning for different cultures around the world.

Around the globe, the presence of numerous places such as archaeological sites, churches, and temples, built for the purpose of aligning the sunrise of the solstice with specific architectural elements, is physical evidence of the mystical significance attributed to this phase of the year. The essence of this time is closely linked to the celebration of nature, since on this day the energy asks us to celebrate the Sun's power and the richness of the Earth, which brings its ripe fruits into the world.

Mother Earth generously showers the world with gifts to reward all our efforts and devotion.

The prince of our celebrations, the Sun, is born embracing the energy of Cancer, the sign ruled by deep emotions and connected to the element of water, an element that is very important to this festival, as it is believed that in the night preceding the solstice, the dew absorbs the magic of dawn and acquires the power to vanquish all negativity; hence its use in cleansing baths.

Simultaneously, fire takes on a crucial role because, according to some European lore, during this night the gates between the material world and the immaterial one become thinner, allowing spirits to contact living beings; therefore, bonfires are built to ward off misfortune and awaken the ardor in men's hearts.

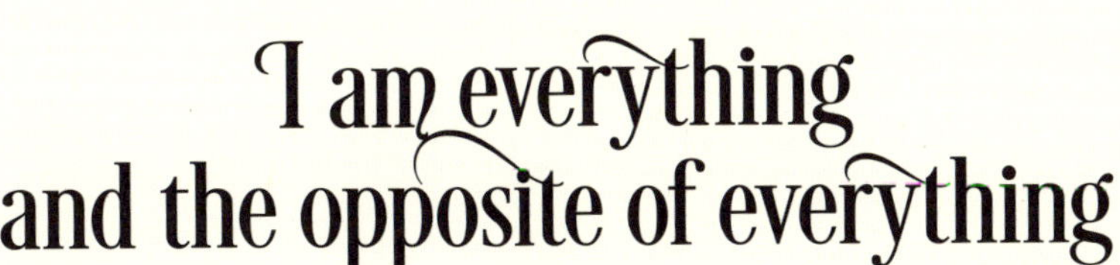

I am everything and the opposite of everything

✦ ✦ ✦

FROM ITS HEAVENLY THRONE, the Sun of the solstice triumphs over the world, guiding and inspiring the soul of every living being. This festival celebrates the extraordinary life force that animates us and allows us to achieve great things when we harness our energy and willpower.

Reaching a goal speaks to the satisfaction of having achieved a substantive result; yet it brings with it the awareness that a new challenge is soon to follow. This eternal binary cycle is what enables us to grow and evolve.

Nothing is ever static; every day is a new challenge. Everything in this universe is always perfectly in balance.

It is exactly in the opposition between extroversion and introspection that the true meaning of this day lies. We must learn to celebrate our victories, yet it is also crucial to consolidate the wisdom we have acquired, so as not to render our entire journey pointless.

On a magical level, the solstice represents this transformation. Our ego from raw material turns into precious metal because it has been tempered by our consciousness; yet, despite this, we still have not reached the end of our journey.

Our life changes continuously. We must understand that every time an obstacle arises before us, we are given the chance to grow, because our soul is destined for greatness and—challenge after challenge—we shall prevail.

Everywhere we can see that magic is ready to give us all the support we need; during these days, magic plants are loaded with power, and the elements eagerly await to be called upon in our rituals. Everything supports us in this phase; our task is to open up to these beautiful powers.

Abundance and purification

✦ ✦ ✦

THE MONTH'S ENERGY

In early June, the days continue to get longer and the Sun warms the charged atmosphere. The warm season prompts us to be outdoors, to enjoy the company of others, and to celebrate life joyfully and lightheartedly. Despite the month's propulsive energy, June also offers moments of quiet and introspection. Sun-filled days can provide the opportunity to reflect on ourselves, our goals, and the path we are undertaking, and whether what we are creating in our lives matches our desires.

FULL MOON

The full Moon in the period connected to Litha represents a time in which we can ask for what we need to fulfill our existence, without greed.

Summon magical forces to perform rituals for abundance.

This energy is symbolized by honey, the product of the labor of the industrious bee, a creature linked to the deities of various pantheons. Use honey in your celebration by adding this special ingredient to a dessert you will share with your friends. Don't forget to share some of it with the fairies, by placing a piece on the windowsill overnight.

NEW MOON

The new Moon, with its energy of renewal, is a perfect match for the purifying power of the solstice, creating a favorable opportunity to liberate oneself of negative energy weighing one down and preventing one from focusing on one's real potential.

During this phase, devote yourself to performing rituals to cleanse negative energy.

To this end, Hypericum can be a valuable ally in the process. Place some of these golden blooms inside a bag and store it under your pillow to promote sleep and ward off nightmares.

Accepting one's duality

✦ ✦ ✦

WITH THE OPPOSITION between longest day and shortest night, the solstice symbolizes the duality that exists in nature and the universe.

Concentrate and answer the questions that most resonate with your soul.

✦ ***In a clearing, you meet an elderly lady who turns out to be a witch. You have the chance to get one of her charms. Which do you choose?***

A. A potion to remove all the obstacles in your life.
B. A magical bag that will improve your finances.

✦ ***You can finally decorate your dream home without constraints to your creativity and desires. What are your must-haves?***

A. A cozy fireplace and a huge bathtub.
B. A gigantic library and luxury furnishings.

✦ ***During a moonless night, you are walking along a deserted path when suddenly a spirit appears before you. They are benevolent and do not wish to harm you. What would they look like?***

A. An ethereal spirit resembling a woman with long red hair.
B. A playful woodland spirit in the likeness of a young goblin.

✦ ***You decide to organize a dinner with your closest friends. Your task is to select the venue. Where do you go?***

A. An ethnic restaurant where you can taste spicy, flavorful dishes.
B. A traditional restaurant that serves simple dishes with genuine ingredients.

✦ ***If you were to describe your biggest flaw, it would be:***

A. Your emotions, which often get in the way of your life and your choices.
B. Your thoughts: you often get distracted and you fail to focus on one thing at a time.

YOU ANSWERED MOSTLY "A": THE POWER OF FIRE, THE INTUITION OF WATER

The vigor of fire must be tempered by the wisdom of water

✦ ✦ ✦

Fire, symbol of energy, burns vigorously, lighting your path and propelling you to action. Water represents calm, fluidity, and empathy; it is welcoming and nourishing; it allows you to flow and connect with others. These apparently opposing elements are actually complementary and dependent on one another. Without water, fire would risk burning out of control; and without fire, water would stagnate, becoming motionless and frozen. Likewise, your power is guided by this duality: you need to learn to act insightfully and think before acting, weighing up the consequences of your choices and considering others' points of view.

Recommended ritual: meditating on the spirit.

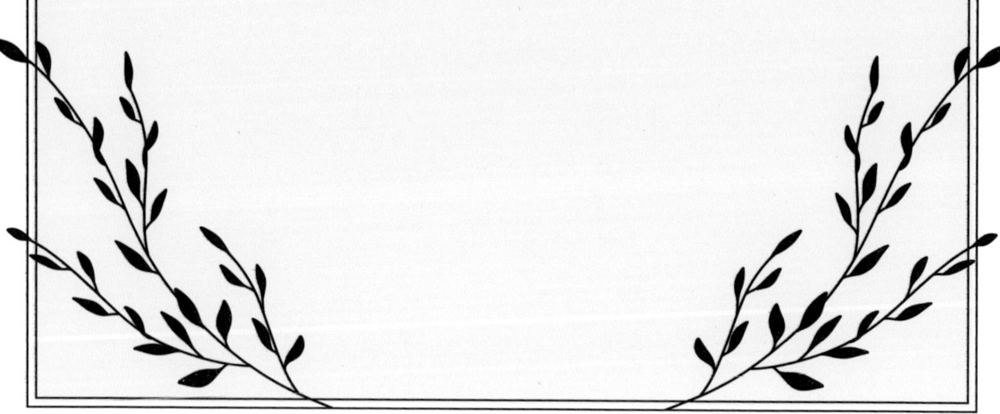

YOU ANSWERED MOSTLY "B":
THE STABILITY OF THE EARTH, THE CREATIVITY OF THE AIR

With the solidity of the Earth, your dreams take shape

✦ ✦ ✦

Earth and air are two essential elements that sustain and inspire us.

The Earth represents stability and concreteness, while the air is light and changeable and represents free thinking and creativity. These two elements complement and depend on one another just as a dream would never be actualized without concrete action; likewise, our soul seeks balance. Your spirit is reminding you that trivial thoughts can be a source of inspiration; however, taking action to turn them into reality is key. Don't be afraid to reach for the stars with your imagination; just remember that the power to achieve your dreams lies in steadfastness and perseverance.

Recommended ritual: the golden call of prosperity.

Summer's symphony of nature

✦ ✦ ✦

The Litha festival is a time when energies dance around us, and a few simple actions are the way to fully experience these sensations.

PURIFICATION: THE PURITY OF WATER AND FLOWERS

According to pagan tradition, the moment in which the solstice Sun is born, herbs and water become charged with magic powers.

SUPPLIES: A glass bowl, water, essential oil, rose petals, lavender, and St. John's wort. Take extra care in case you suffer from any allergies.

METHOD: On the night before the solstice, place the bowl outside and fill it with the flowers and a few drops of essential oil. Notice the beautiful colors that nature has gifted you, inhale the intoxicating scent that is released when the flowers come into contact with the crystal-clear water. Pour the water into the bowl and leave it uncovered overnight and for part of the morning. To prevent any insects from coming into contact with it, you can cover the bowl with a natural-fiber cloth. The next day, wash your body from the feet up to the head, using the water from the bowl; as you pour it, visualize the light of the solstice penetrating you, and its golden power warding off darkness and negativity. Follow this by mentally reciting your spell:

The energy of the Earth purifies me, nourishes me.
Darkness no longer has any power; light illuminates my path.

Devote all the time you need to this phase and, once all the negative energy has been eliminated from your body, take a relaxing warm bath.

TRANSMUTATION: MEDITATING ON THE SPIRIT

Meditation is a practice that elevates your spirit and restores peace of mind. It can be applied as often as you need.

SUPPLIES: Relaxing music with natural sounds, and a quiet and comfortable place where you can lie down.

METHOD: After having created a pleasant environment by filling it with music, lie down. Breathing slowly, let go of tensions and worries. Now close your eyes and, in your mind, visualize a clearing. Start with a simple image like a blade of grass. Do not try controlling your thoughts: let them glide past, like clouds in the sky. Notice the feeling of peace permeating the place you are in; explore the depths of your being and the power hidden in your inner dimension. Take your time. Rest. Reset.

Before leaving the place you are in, say this sentence to express your gratitude:

Respectfully, I leave;
I am grateful for every gift,
whether large or small.

Focus on your physical body and center yourself. In your initial attempts, you may lose concentration or visualize only a few details. Do not be discouraged: it's normal, and you need to persevere. Repeat this practice regularly, and your skills will improve, providing unique experiences and reinvigorating your personal power.

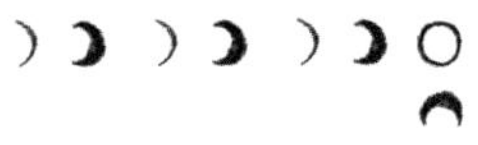

ABUNDANCE: THE GOLDEN CALL OF PROSPERITY

As mentioned earlier, in many traditions like Ancient Egypt, honey is considered an ingredient with magical and healing powers. Due to its physical and nutritional properties, it is utilized in spells to attract abundance.

SUPPLIES: A resealable glass jar, honey, two ears of wheat, four bay leaves, a yellow natural candle.

METHOD: Before beginning the spell, wash the jar with water and salt and then light the candle. Place your herbs in the jar, visualizing their respective magical correlations. The laurel, symbol of triumph and celebrating success; the wheat, symbol of Mother Earth's abundance. After completing this step, start pouring the honey, taking care not to spill any outside the jar; and recite:

Golden nectar gifted by Mother Earth,
in you flows life itself,
the essence of abundance in me manifests.

Notice the golden honey covering your magic herbs and take the time to repeat your spell until you feel you have charged it with positive energy. Now tightly screw the lid on and hide your visualization charm in your home, making sure it won't be opened until your wishes have come true. To be safe, store it in a box or wrapped in cloth.

The path from Litha to Lammas

✦ ✦ ✦

THE CHANGE THAT LEADS US TO LAMMAS is characterized by the arrival of a new energetic phase. Reaching its peak, the Sun is now aware that it will have to give way to darkness; during this transition, it awakens our desire to connect with our surroundings.

We are always in contact with Mother Earth.
We walk on her,
eat her gifts, and actively
participate in her energetic flow.

Every moment of our life is intertwined with the rhythm of nature. Our bodies are composed of her elements, and our life cycle mirrors that of the seasons.

The reason for recognizing this deep connection is not only to appreciate the natural world's beauty, but also to take responsibility in preserving it. Becoming a conscious steward of Mother Earth means respecting her resources, honoring her cycles, and living harmoniously alongside her.

The connection to Earth is a path to getting back to experiencing magic and our true nature.

The main theme of this phase is:
The energy of the universe dances and resonates within you.
This is a time to rejoice.

To fully embrace this energy, here's what you can do:

✦ Spend time in nature, immersing yourself in its beauty and peace.
✦ Appreciate yourself; start your day with a compliment to boost your self-esteem.
✦ To nourish your soul, devote time to having fun.
✦ Establish a magic atmosphere in your home by using natural scents.
✦ Seek the magic in everything around you.
✦ Eat fresh fruit and vegetables to fuel your body with Mother Earth's gifts.

Remember: Every human being is connected to the natural power. Our duty is to guard, preserve, and nurture it.

Lammas

✦ ✦ ✦

LUNASA

JULY 31—AUGUST 1–2

The reaping of wisdom

✦ ✦ ✦

In August's awakening, when the golden fields sway under the weight of the ripe wheat, the first harvest sabbat is celebrated. This is a magical moment in which two ancient traditions intertwine: Lunasa, the Celtic festival of the Sun god Lugh; and Lammas, the Anglo-Saxon festival of the harvest's end.

With its Celtic roots, Lunasa celebrates the beginning of the harvest, giving thanks to the land for its generosity and acknowledging the sacredness of the seasons' cycles. Lammas, on the other hand, takes its name from *"loaf-mass"* or "feast of bread," recalling the custom of bringing the harvest's first loaf of bread to church to be blessed.

Despite their different roots, the two traditions bear a common thread: both unite in celebrating wheat, a divine symbol of sustenance.

The grain of wheat embodies the essence of this tradition. A portion will be utilized for bread-making and food, while another will be kept for sowing, to ensure the continuity of the life cycle.

In many civilizations, when the fields were plowed, an unharvested section was offered to the nature spirits; today, such tributes to natural entities and similar customs still resonate in every corner of the world.

This period is awash with countless festivals expressing deep gratitude for the gifts of the Earth, given that the harvest represents sustenance and expresses the toil and labor committed throughout the year. Celebrating all this is a way not only to rejoice, but also to motivate; seeing the results we have reaped is encouraging and propels us to keep working and pursuing our goals with renewed energy.

Through gratitude I set my spirit free

✦ ✦ ✦

DESPITE THE PASSING OF TIME, THIS SABBAT STILL BRINGS WITH IT THE ANCIENT LORE linked to nature's cycles, which—having reached this phase of the year—manifests in a concrete way the importance of sacrificing the divine to keep the balance.

In some traditions, this symbolism is embodied by a natural deity destined to be sacrificed to guarantee the continuity of life on Earth. Such spirit, nourished by the summer solstice's solar force, follows a path of transformation, reaching Lammas to then sacrifice its life to ensure the sustenance of humankind. The concept of sacrifice recurs in many cultures around the world; through rituals, myths, and legends, it represents the idea of giving up something precious to benefit someone or the greater good.

Sacrifice is not the cause of suffering,
but an act guided by neighborly love.

In modern celebrations, neopagans prepare offerings of bread, sweets, wheat, corn, sunflowers, and flour, creating a dance of giving and receiving.

As living beings, we need to be aware that we are part of a universal energy cycle; we pick up energy from our surroundings and can transform and distribute it around the world.

Giving is not limited to the sharing of material goods; every action creates a positive ripple that disperses throughout the universe. By helping others, we help ourselves.

Gratitude and gifting allow us to embrace the universe's abundance and share it; in this mutual exchange lies this festival's true wisdom.

Each of us has the power to change things. Together, we can shape a bright and harmonious future for everyone.

I journey toward inner freedom

✦ ✦ ✦

THE MONTH'S ENERGY

While nature explodes with color and vitality, the call of Mother Earth resonates as the bearer of wisdom and infinite possibility. In this period, which marks the transition between the end of July and the month of August, we are given the opportunity to free ourselves of old and limiting mindsets. During this phase of greater freedom, it would be appropriate to take time for one's quality of life, so as to restore both the body and mind that have worked tirelessly throughout the year.

FULL MOON

In this phase, the full Moon occurs at a time when nature's energy is pulsating and alive, which is why we are asked to learn to recognize the presence of this power in our lives.

At this time of the year, you may devote yourself to working with the natural energy and its spirits.

Walk barefoot on grass or dirt to enable you to tune into the soil's energy and feel nature's vibrations more deeply. Surround yourself with unspoiled nature.

NEW MOON

August's energy connects the magic practice of the new Moon with the use of plants, given that, during these days, the power of nature provides ingredients laden with magic.

In this lunar phase, it is important to devote yourself to energetically cleansing your spirit.

Lavender is a wonderful plant with calming and purifying properties, and it triumphs in August. Its purple color relates to royalty and subtle energy; it is considered a magic and sacred plant.

Add a few drops of lavender essential oil to an aromatherapy diffuser. Besides spreading a calming and cleansing scent through the room, it will help elevate your spiritual energy during your daily practice.

Inner growth and self-actualization

✦ ✦ ✦

Nature gives us hints on how to practice gratitude and tap into the positive powers around us; we need to learn how to attract it and which parts of ourselves to nurture.

Concentrate and answer the questions that most resonate with your soul.

✦ ***After walking through a maze, you arrive at an old door. You open it. Inside it you find:***

A. Access to a secret garden.

B. An expensive room with luxurious furnishings.

✦ ***You go on vacation with friends. When you have to choose a destination, you act based on your instincts and buy a ticket for:***

A. A mountain village surrounded by nature where you can go on walks and spend time in complete silence.

B. A seaside resort where you can spend time on unadulterated fun, spending time in night-clubs until dawn.

✦ ***Which divination tool would you choose to foretell the future?***

A. A tarot reading lit by the flickering flames of scented candles.

B. A fascinating reading of coffee grounds, a window on destiny that opens with every sip.

✦ ***Contact with nature is different for each of us. What does it mean to you?***

A. A moment to rest, relax, and contemplate the beauty of your surroundings.

B. An opportunity to take long walks to release energy and stress.

✦ ***Choose which soundscape will accompany your meditation:***

A. You immerse yourself in the sound of nature, where the chirping of birds intertwines with the whispering of the wind.

B. You surrender to the shamanic drum's hypnotic rhythm.

YOU ANSWERED MOSTLY "A":
THE FOREST'S INSIGHT

Everything is connected, and in our soul's silence we rediscover ourselves

✦ ✦ ✦

The forest, with its peaceful and evocative atmosphere, inspires a sense of sacredness and mystery. It is a setting in which we are humbled by nature's vastness, where we can establish a bond with something greater.

Life in the forest represents a concrete example of harmony and interdependence between all living things: each element plays a crucial role in keeping the balance within the ecosystem.

Returning to live harmoniously with ourselves and the planet is fundamental, because everything in the world moves at its own pace. Our task is to reinstate understanding through calm.

Recommended ritual: Earth charm.

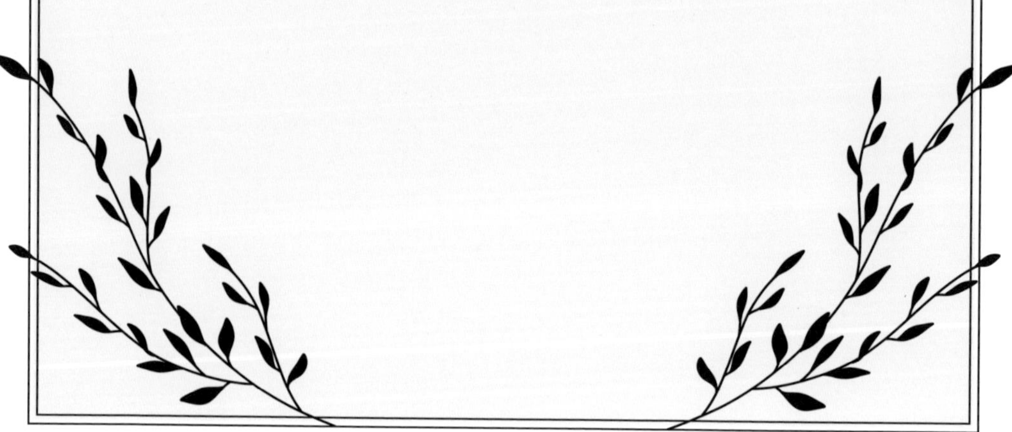

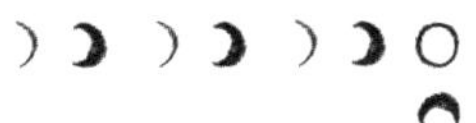

YOU ANSWERED MOSTLY "B":
GRAIN ENERGY

Even a tiny grain can tip the scale

✦ ✦ ✦

A grain of wheat, although small and apparently insignificant, holds enormous potential; with the correct lighting conditions, water, and nutrition, the seed germinates, develops roots in the soil, and grows into a sturdy ear.

Similarly, each of us is born with infinite potential within ourselves.

We can grow, learn, evolve, and accomplish great feats; however, to blossom we need spiritual nurturing, deep bonds, and a fertile ground in which to establish roots.

Along our spiritual journey, like wheat we reap the fruits of our inner work. Gratitude for our progress and our experiences nourishes us, spurring us to continue pursuing our spiritual journey; thus, it is fundamental that we do not lose heart so as not to make our efforts futile.

Recommended ritual: attracting courage.

The magic of Mother Earth

✦ ✦ ✦

To work with the energy of this time of year, we need to understand the importance of renewing the connection and balance with nature through every action.

CONNECTION: EARTH CHARM

The witch knows the importance of interconnectedness with the Earth's power. This ritual will allow us to make a charm to enhance our awareness and commitment to this bond.

SUPPLIES: A white plate, some soil, seeds, corn kernels, flower petals of your choice, a pendant.

METHOD: This ritual can be performed either indoors or outdoors; for improved effectiveness, choose a natural environment.

Put the soil on the plate as a base, then arrange the seeds in a spiral shape. Do this by working from the outside in, thus attracting the energy toward the center of the symbol.

Next, complete the design by adding the corn and flower petals. Finally, as you decorate the spiral, allow your creativity to freely express itself.

Now place the pendant at the center and say:

Mother Earth, powerful and ancient,
intertwine my soul with your vital cycles.
Ancestral power, guide my journey,
your magic I attract, O divine spirit.

Close your eyes and clear your mind. Gently place one hand on your pendant. Imagine a vibrant current of energy emerging from the depths of the Earth, saturating the necklace and becoming an integral part of it.

Now open your eyes and, as a sign of gratitude and respect, sow the seeds you have received.

PERSONAL STRENGTH: ATTRACTING COURAGE

Certain times in our lives require great courage on our part. This simple spell can help us reclaim our missing strength.

SUPPLIES: A glass bowl, water, a candlestick, an orange candle, a needle, dried thyme.

METHOD: Fill the glass bowl with water and thyme. Let it rest overnight under the crescent Moon.

In a quiet place, arrange everything you need before you.

Using the needle, engrave the word "courage" on the candle and, if you like, embellish it with other symbols depicting the strength you wish to attract.

Avoiding the wick, pour a few drops of the magic water over the candle.

Recite the spell:

Fruit of the Earth's power,
for my purpose I bless you.
You are the conduit, the call;
give me courage and strength.

Light the candle on the candlestick. Feel its energy spreading throughout your body and recharging your soul. Visualize your spirit now becoming brave and confident.

Wait as long as you need; allow yourself to be dowsed by the fire's energy and the thyme's wisdom. When the timing is right, blow the candle out and store it in a special place.

Repeat this ritual whenever you require courage, like in a challenging situation. Remember that the true power resides in you, dormant.

BLOCKAGE: THE SEAL OF THE NAILS AND THE SUN

Nails, especially antique ones, are a traditional element in European magic and folklore. Sharp objects are commonly used in magic rituals for protection purposes. The nail is associated with the ability to repel unwanted energy.

SUPPLIES: Three nails, a black natural fiber bag, a red woolen string.

METHOD: On a cloudless day, expose the nails to sunlight at the hottest time of the day and leave them for two hours. The metal will need to cool slightly because, in doing so, the nails will symbolically be saturated with the solar energy that we will use for our spell.

After this ritual, go to a secluded place and put the nails inside the bag. Proceed slowly, one at a time, and recite the following words for each:

The Sun has blessed the metal,
now this magic object is enchanted and
energized by my words.
No negative energy shall pass through it.

Once the process is completed, close the bag using the red woolen string, wrapping it around the bag and tying everything up with three knots. Next, you'll need to hang the bag from a door or window to keep the powers at bay. You can make this spell every time you feel the need to protect the energy of your home.

The path from Lammas to Mabon

✦ ✦ ✦

THE KEY TO THIS PHASE is understanding the importance of looking after ourselves and our spiritual healing.

The sign concomitant with this transformation is Virgo. Its energy, linked to perfectionism and a tendency to analyze everything, if taken to the extreme could hinder our quest for connection with the divine. Instead, our task will be to apply its teachings, because the awareness of having all the answers will help us be humble and open to learning and discovery.

Spiritual healing is a complex and multifaceted process that involves different dimensions in the human being.

It is a personal journey aimed at restoring harmony and balance between body, mind, and soul, promoting the general well-being of the individual.

The main theme of this phase is:
We approach the divine with much humility and openness.
Like a seed in the dark Earth, our soul awaits.

To fully embrace this energy, here's what you can do:

- ✦ Choose a specific time of day to devote to your spiritual practice, even if just for a few minutes.
- ✦ Learn to forgive yourself. We are imperfect. At this stage, be more patient with yourself.
- ✦ Surround yourself with positive people.
- ✦ Pursue a hobby you have neglected for a while.
- ✦ Start organizing a secret place for storing your magic herbs.
- ✦ Place symbols of the Moon around your home to attract its energy during your magic practice.
- ✦ Cyclically purify your home with natural incense.

Remember: Do not hesitate, because confidence is your most powerful asset. Self-belief is already half the battle to realizing your dreams.

✦ ✦ ✦

FALL EQUINOX

SEPTEMBER 20–21–22

I am the echo of those who came before me

✦ ✦ ✦

THE EARTH IS TINGED IN GOLDEN HUES as the atmosphere begins to change, marking the arrival of the second harvest festival: the fall equinox.

In the Northern Hemisphere, this arrives between September 21 and 23; and this stage in the Wheel of the Year is called Mabon, a term coined in the 20th century to indicate the sabbat that coincides with the arrival of the fall equinox, which is linked to the god of youth, hunting, plant life, and crops (Modron's son in Welsh mythology).

At this time, we devote ourselves once again to celebrating nature's bounty and our hard work, aware that the dark phase of the year is inching closer.

Like its opposite, Ostara, the spring equinox, in this phase we also witness a moment of balance, of harmonious union between contrasting forces.

At the beginning of fall, the mystic meaning of the harvest is deeper than the simple act of gathering produce; we are heading toward the last stage of a long journey that commenced with nurturing the land and respecting nature and its rhythms, an often-communal journey, rooted in history, intertwining our actions with those of our ancestors. The fall equinox prompts us to feel the deep connection with those who preceded us by stepping on the same soil that welcomed their steps. Nowadays, what we admire in our landscape is the echo of their actions: the road that guides us, the house that welcomes us, the protected forest, the cultivated field. Every day, and especially today, we sense our ancestors' tangible presence within ourselves and the places we inhabit.

Sacrifice and wisdom

✦ ✦ ✦

THIS SEASON'S COLORS ARE PURE POETRY for our soul; in this phase of the year, we begin to understand that death is an important stage in the entire natural cycle. The leaves fall because the trees, aware of the impending arrival of the harsh winter, abandon what is no longer necessary to preserve their lifeblood. This sacrifice, which the plant kingdom repeats year after year, is mirrored in the animal world. Since prehistoric times, hunting took on a sacred meaning as the hunter ventured into the wilderness to procure food for his village. The animal sacrificed its life, acknowledging the hunter's skill and contributing to the community's livelihood.

In this circle of life and death, this sacrifice represents respect and interconnection between living beings.

The sacrifice was never gratuitous, but constituted a deliberate act carried out for the common good, to ensure the survival through winter and beyond. It was a privilege and an honor to have this kill; and if it failed, the cause would be sought in the village's attitude toward the nature spirits or the merciless gods. Mabon asks us to reflect on what we have sown and what we have reaped, not only in terms of material goods, but also in terms of experiences, emotions, and learnings. Does the harvest reflect our aspirations? What helped its growth, and what hindered it? In periods under the influence of the equinox's power, understanding is a fundamental component in balancing one's energy in the right direction. This is the only way possible for us to grow and evolve on our spiritual journey.

Balance and strength

✦ ✦ ✦

THE MONTH'S ENERGY

Mabon is connected to Libra, the zodiac sign characterized by an innate sense of justice, harmony, and a constant quest for balance. This sign's energy shows us that at this time of the year, we must commit to resolving conflict through compromise, without jeopardizing our values and identity. Opting for a calm approach doesn't mean giving in to others; it's a wise way to avoid unnecessary conflict that could waste our time and energy, both of which are valuable gifts that we must guard jealously.

FULL MOON

September's full Moon prompts us to commit to improving our wisdom. The apple in Western tradition is a powerful symbol of knowledge and self-awareness, which is why we shall use it for our spell.

During this full Moon, ask to receive messages to enrich your spirit, through your dreams.

When there is a full Moon, cut an apple in half and place a bay leaf inside it, on which you will have written a question. Close the apple with a natural thread and leave it outside, in the moonlight, overnight; the next day, you can bury it.

NEW MOON

Oil has great cleansing and blessing properties, preparing a blend charged by the new Moon will allow you to use it in your magic practice.

During this phase, we prepare an oil to enhance our connection with our ancestors.

Into a bottle pour some water, olive oil, three drops of cypress essential oil, and a teaspoon of tobacco. Expose the ingredients to the new Moon. You can use this water as an offering to your ancestors, to call their attention to your prayers. Do not ingest.

What must I protect myself from?

AT THIS STAGE OF THE YEAR, we find ourselves on a very introspective path, so it is helpful to ascertain what our weak points could be, to be able to skillfully avoid attracting negative energy that could weigh down our spirit.

✦ ***If you could express your talent through a dream job, what career would you choose?***

A. You would take care of people, a job to assist the community.
B. A job that would afford you time to calmly express your ideas.

✦ ***Which situation best describes you in a romantic relationship?***

A. My loved one's opinion is most important, I listen to their advice and try to put it into practice so I can improve.
B. I know what I want in a relationship, and it must align with my values. One should not have to settle in love.

✦ ***You find yourself among strangers. Everyone is looking at you. What are they thinking?***

A. They are judging me. At first glance I tend to stand out.
B. No one knows me. I must introduce myself and try to befriend someone.

✦ ***You need to perform a ritual during the night of a full Moon. How do you proceed?***

A. You seek out some books for advice on what to do and follow each step.
B. The most important thing is not the ritual: it's not being discovered. I must be very careful.

✦ ***A group of witches invites you to join their group. What do you do?***

A. I accept gladly. They will be able to teach me many interesting things I do not know yet; I need them.
B. I decline. I prefer to practice alone, focusing on my energy and my personal spiritual-awakening.

YOU ANSWERED MOSTLY "A":
PROTECT YOURSELF FROM EXTERNAL POWERS

By always listening to others, we forget the sound of our own voice

✦ ✦ ✦

Humans are social beings and often seek out a group to be part of. Instinct leads us to interact with the outside world and to assess our spirit according to society's values.

Being humble can be very useful, yet we must always bear in mind that people do not always have the same intentions as us. What we may do joyfully and with a community spirit, in others may be just an attempt to gain a personal advantage.

Our standards are not universal, which is why we must learn to look at situations objectively. The opinion of others matters; however, we must learn to fight our own battles if we believe in them, provided they cause no harm.

Recommended ritual: the decision of the arcane.

YOU ANSWERED MOSTLY "B":

PROTECT YOURSELF FROM INTERNAL POWERS

Even the most beautiful jewel fails to shine when locked in a safe

✦ ✦ ✦

It is natural to believe that one's opinion is the most valid, yet it is crucial to be open to discussions and different outlooks. This is useful in the right quantity.

Respecting one's identity is an important aspect of defining one's strength. Just remember that in this world, one cannot act as if one were completely detached from society.

It's okay to protect oneself from external hate, but how do we protect ourselves from the self? The main flaw in being square is having edges. As long as we only use our personal criteria, we will feed both our strengths and our weaknesses, which could lead to stagnation. Let's open ourselves to the world, just a little.

Recommended ritual: the call of peace.

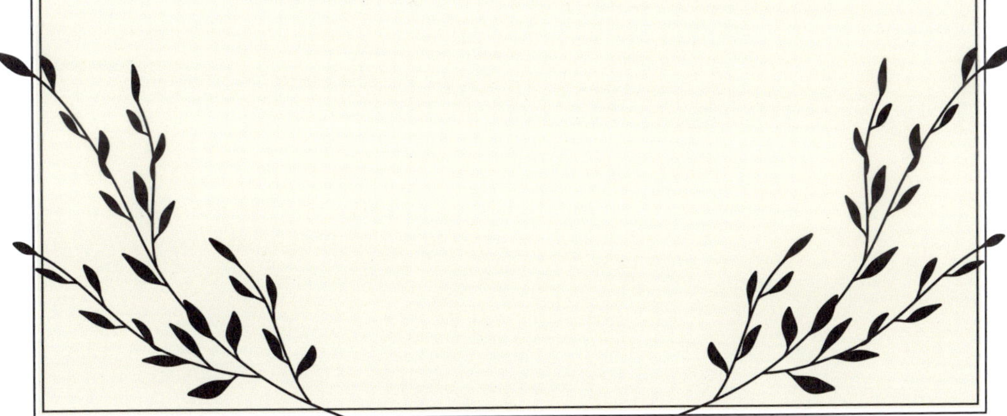

The melancholic beauty

✦ ✦ ✦

The fall equinox is full of magic traditions the purpose of which is to nourish our spirit and give us the tools to better face the challenges ahead.

CELEBRATION: THE ACORN OF GOOD FORTUNE

In the lore of the Germanic peoples, the acorn was considered sacred; not merely a seed, it symbolized wealth and power, because all the power of the majestic oak was concentrated within it.

SUPPLIES: Acorns, a candle, a plate.

METHOD: In the fall, take a walk to collect the acorns lying on the ground. The main thing is to have an odd number. You may perform this ritual during the equinox or the waxing Moon.

Place the acorns on a large enough dish and discard any damaged ones. Ensure that none is overlapping and that they all look nice.

Now light the candle and, taking great care, slowly circle clockwise over the dish, and slightly tilt the candle so the melted wax begins to drip.

As you proceed, recite your spell three times while still circling:

Luck, luck, I call you back,
now show your hand.
Show me your decision,
which are the gifts you will accept.

Pay close attention to this spell, because the drops of wax will begin to drip onto some of the acorns, blessing them. Blow out the candle and only use the acorns with a wax residue on them. These can be used as amulets. You can take them with you or place them inside your home to attract good luck.

JUSTICE: THE DECISION OF THE ARCANE

Justice is a tarot card: we use its power to attract the powers of the universe in those situations in which we need the intervention of the universe to balance the energy. This spell cannot be used to cause harm to others.

SUPPLIES: The Tarot card of Justice (if you don't have Tarot cards, print out an image that represents it), and a glass of wine.

METHOD: To carry out this spell, your intent is of the utmost importance, as well as how much you wish to restore balance.

Position the Tarot's arcana and place the glass of wine between you and the card.

Take your time to clear your mind, concentrate on what you want to ask, and reconsider the situation mentally without letting your emotions get the better of you. Right now, you cannot feel any anger.

Now raise the glass and, as you approach it, whisper your spell over it:

Justice, infallible balance,
I summon your attention at this moment.
Listen to my words: restore balance.

Describe the situation for which you seek justice. Don't be afraid of going into detail: reveal everything. Once you've completed your description, finish with "So be it."

Leave the Tarot card in front of the wine glass overnight; the next day, pour the wine outside, aware that the universe is already in motion.

CALM: THE CALL OF PEACE

Amethyst is the guardian of peace and harmony; in crystal therapy, it brings serenity to the spirit by balancing the mind. Let's create a charm that we can wear at the most challenging times in our lives, as a tool for keeping calm.

SUPPLIES: An amethyst pendant, a bowl of distilled water, incense.

METHOD: Take the amethyst pendant and immerse it in the bowl of water for a few minutes. Visualize the water transforming into a vortex of cleansing energy, absorbing any negativity and impurities that may have attached to the crystal. Gently remove the pendant from the water and dry it with a clean cloth.

Pass the pendant through the incense smoke, visualizing how it penetrates every part of the stone, purifying it. Imagine that the smoke is a cloak enveloping the amethyst and giving it new life and power.

Now it's time to ask the crystal for its assistance: hold it in your hands. Breathe air into your lungs, then exhale by blowing over the pendant. Repeat this step at least three times, remaining calm as you do this.

Now recite your spell:

Amethyst, gem of light and mystery,
dissolve stress and anxiety with your touch.
Bring inner calm before me:
this pendant is now blessed.

Wear your charm whenever you face a stressful situation. Hold it in your hands to summon its power.

The path from Mabon to Samhain

✦ ✦ ✦

THE PATH THAT TAKES SHAPE AFTER MABON leads us directly to Samhain, one of the most important festivals in the Wheel of the Year. For this reason, during this transition, we are asked to pay close attention to the energy around us. Our journey begins with the energy of Libra inviting us to find and transform imbalances into opportunities for growth, then reaches Scorpio, the main symbol of transformation and connection to the emotions.

This part of our journey will lead us into the dark cave of the subconscious and our spiritual essence.

Scorpio is a sign deeply connected to the spirit world and the past. At this time, it is especially helpful to start connecting with one's ancestors, asking them for guidance and support.

The main theme of this phase is:
We may be afraid of darkness, but it will remain so only until we have the courage to illuminate it with our strength.

Here's what we can do to manage the flow of these energies:

- ✦ Start researching your roots; build your family tree.
- ✦ Follow your instinct to identify what energies are currently around you.
- ✦ Be mindful with your every action, without allowing a fear of the future to distract you.
- ✦ Regularly cleanse your home by cleaning the surfaces with salt and water.
- ✦ Diffuse a soothing essential oil while you work or study.
- ✦ Examine your priorities: consider what is important to you in life.
- ✦ Start testing your practice using the protection spells.

Remember: The universe is constantly in equilibrium. Do not shy away from challenges, or you will face obstacles that you can only overcome with effort.

FEDERICA VANINI

AKA Incanto del Corvo, Federica is an independent scholar who has been delving into the roots of Italian folk magic for years. Her passion for nature and her grandmother's teachings have guided her along a path of studies and practices connected to divination, magic traditions, and natural power. Nowadays, through her Instagram page, she shares her knowledge and inspires many enthusiasts.

ERICA BRUCOLI

Born and living in Turin, Erica is a graphic artist and illustrator who moves through the world in search of inspiration. Nature is her main muse, but her ideas also emerge from the pages of books, along with art, travel, and mysticism. Thanks to years of experience in the fashion industry, she has honed her artistic sensibility and developed a unique vision. After graduating in editorial illustration at Milan's MiMaster, Erica has dedicated herself fully to her passion, working as an illustrator and graphic artist and continuing to make art.

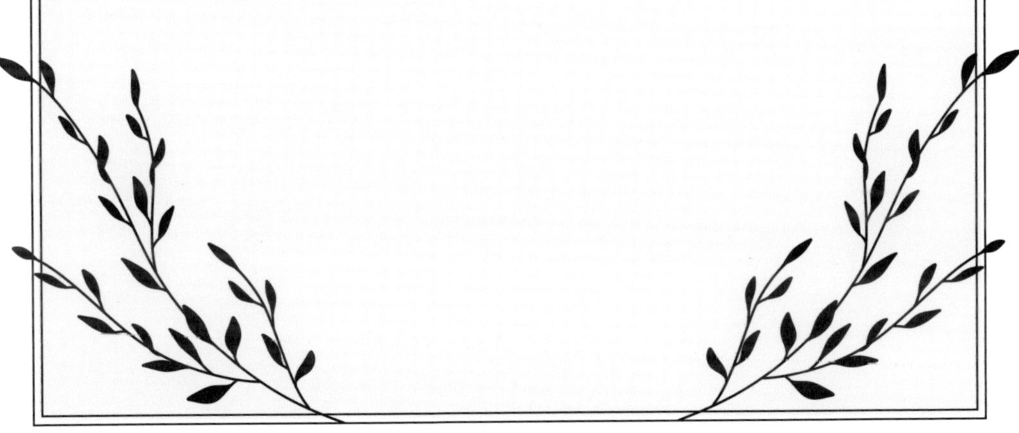